What People About This Book...

Francie Willis, CEO The Urban Retreat

"The Urban Retreat focuses on physical replenishment but in addition to our bodies, we also have a spirit that cries out for a greater purpose to our lives than just getting through the day. This book is so much more than the birth story of Inspire Women. It uses a specific story to tell the greater need for all of us to connect with God's greater purpose which continues regardless of the tragedies and setbacks we experience. I recommend this book to anyone who is serious about discovering the reason God created us and the work He has entrusted to each of us to finish."

Donna Fujimoto Cole, CEO Cole Chemical

"It takes vision to see something wonderful before anyone else sees it. It takes courage to keep fighting for the dream when the odds are against you. It takes compassion to live for a cause that is bigger than yourself. This book is about mercy, courage, faith to believe God will intervene miraculously, and the tenacity to keep going until the dream becomes a reality."

Sue Burnett, CEO Burnett Staffing Specialists

"As one who specializes in personnel placement, I know what it means to put the right person in the right assignment. This book is about God's personnel organization as He hand picks and trains His servants to fulfill His purpose. It opened my eyes to see that life is more than doing a job. It's about living a calling and serving God's divine appointments with passion and excellence."

When Dreams Won't Die

The Autobiography and Birth Story
of **Inspire Women**

by Anita Carman

Founder & President of Inspire Women

WITH

A Personal Reflection Journal

for You to discover where Your new story begins

IW.WD.V2

ISBN 0-9772905-0-6

SAN 257-1439

Published by **Inspire Women**
6524 San Felipe #516
Houston, Texas 77057
(713)521-1400

*Inspire Women does not accept
unsolicited manuscripts.*

All Scripture quotations are taken from
the New International Version (NIV) of the Bible.

For additional copies of
When Dreams Won't Die
or to contact **Anita Carman** for a
speaking engagement please visit
www.inspirewomen.org
or call (713)521-1400

HOUSTON, TEXAS • USA

Dedication

This book is dedicated to
Inspire Women's
"Secret Charlie"

Who is *"Secret Charlie"*?

Think of Inspire Women as a faith-based *Charlie's Angels* team. While the "Angels" on the T.V. series, *Charlie's Angels*, fought with karate and guns, the women of Inspire Women fight the battles of life with the power of God's Word. In the same way that Charlie in *Charlie's Angels* would protect the "Angels" and gave them what they needed to fight their battles, Inspire Women's *"Secret Charlie"* has underwritten the basic payroll and overhead of the organization to ensure its existence as a gift to the city on a perpetual basis. This support helps the staff to focus their time on ministering to women and to raising the funds for the biblical inspiration and the training of all God's daughters for His purpose.

Inspire Women is grateful for our *"Secret Charlie"*. Thank you for representing the heart of our heavenly Father and for providing a banner of love and protection over us. Thank you for believing in the dreams God entrusted to us and for being a friend who trusts us with God's mission. We honor you as Houston's Father of the Year. You are the best "father" any girl could pray for and we love you with all our heart!

Acknowledgements

My heartfelt thanks to Robert Carman, Ty Herring, Forrest Henson, Jr., and Tim Black. I praise God for godly men who proof-read this book as I was writing. Thank you for encouraging me and for sharing with me how this book touched your heart.

I thank God for Lisa Brown, my friend who is also an attorney. Thank you for taking time during your work break to read this book while trying to hide your tears in the midst of your work environment. I thank God for my friend Shelley Haden. Thank you for sharing how you could not put this book down once you started reading it. I also thank God for Puddie Pitcock, Francie Willis, Bonnie Likover, Julie Jordan, Mia Kang, and Bev Victory for encouraging me to share this book with others.

To Linda Huang, I express my deepest gratitude for the gift of your friendship and talent. Thank you for designing the beautiful bookcover and for laying out the manuscript. More than that, I thank you for connecting your heart with this story. It touched me deeply when you told me you shouldn't have read the book on the plane because you were sobbing right through it. To my friends Joan Turley and Judy Horne, thank you for laughing and crying with me through the pages of this book as you gently probed to help me fill in the missing gaps in the story. Joan, I will never forget when you looked up at me with mascara running down your face, saying, "Where's the comic relief?" Judy, you brought new meaning to the word "unhesitating". This word will always be special to me because of the journey we shared together. The staff at Inspire Women has heard me say this a thousand times and I mean it with all my heart, "Oh the tears will be worth it if someone will be encouraged by this story and find hope in the great God we serve."

In writing this book God brought to mind hundreds of volunteers and supporters, but alas, it was not possible to list every name. If your name was omitted, please know that God has recorded every act of service or love rendered to Him. Please also know that your love meant the world to the women of our city. May Houston's example inspire other cities to bless their women in a similar way!

Contents

THE AUTOBIOGRAPHY

PERSONAL REFLECTION JOURNAL

Introduction

W HAT DO YOU DO WITH A DREAM THAT WON'T DIE? Sometimes, even when all hope for the fulfillment of a dream is gone, your heart still longs for a dream that refuses to be buried. Have you ever felt a groaning deep within you? How do you deal with the years the locusts have eaten or the promise of a future that feels impossible? How do you get out of bed in the morning when you're tired of the charade and you can't go through one more day of faking that everything is all right? Are you discouraged by how your story is unfolding? Are you ready for a new story to begin?

The first time I felt God touch my life, I was 11. I was born in the city of Hong Kong when the country was a British Colony ruled by England. I was in my adolescent years when I experienced major communist uprisings in my city. In order to maintain order, the British government announced a curfew. All residents were to be off the streets by seven in the evening.

One night, when I was already in bed, I heard a blast in the distance. Then came the eerie cry of the mob as they ran down the street with the British army chasing in hot pursuit. There is something very distinctive about the sound of army boots hitting the hard concrete. It felt like a powerful force was overtaking human flesh and blood. As the mob ran past my bedroom window, my body began to tremble. I was sweating under my blankets but I was paralyzed by fear and afraid to throw my blankets off. As the artificial silence returned, I peeked out from under my blanket and looked at the sky through my bedroom window. I marveled at its beauty and the thousands of stars that shone down upon the turbulence in my city. Then out of the mouth of a child came this prayer, "God, if you can see me, if you can find me among the millions in my city, please help me reach the free land of America."

The next day, as I was going down the stairs of our three floor apartment building on my way to school, I saw our neighbor's son. I shifted my eyes downward as I passed him but I noticed his head was shaved. This was how the police marked those who broke curfew. He must have been caught in the streets and now he had been identified visibly by his shaven head.

When I got to the gates of my mission school, I took a deep breath and ran as fast as I could through the entrance. I remembered reading in the paper that the Communists loathed religion and they were leaving bombs at the gates of Christian schools. When I returned home, I would take a breath and run as fast as I could up the stairs while screaming for my mother to open the door. In addition to the political unrest, there was local violence in my neighborhood as well. Just the week before, my friend from school was raped in the stairwell by someone who had been waiting for her.

There were days when I felt life was backing me up

against a wall and that the fear of life would destroy me. It was as if doom was just around the corner and if I was not careful, I would step on a landmine. When I walked past a puddle of blood on the street covered with newspaper, I heard someone had lost hope and jumped from a building. When I watched a little girl tied up in the back alley with her hands behind her back, while the kitchen boys took bets on how many times her mother would strike her, I felt the desperation of victims of abuse.

From an early age, I sensed that God is not the one who hurts us. I was more afraid of fallen humanity than of God. However, I had a problem – at that young age, I didn't know how to draw strength from God.

The dream of coming to America began in my mother's heart. When U.S. Immigration denied my parent's petition to exit the country and her children were leaving on a student visa, my mother became very depressed. I woke up at the age of 17 to discover she had taken her own life. I arrived in this country feeling like an emotional orphan. I had no idea how the story would end.

Years later, as the Founder of Inspire Women, I asked the Lord, "Is this how the story ends?" He answered, "This is where the story begins." All my past was just the preparation. God allowed the pain to stretch my heart to have more compassion. Would I put the rock of God's Word beneath the feet of all His daughters and help them discover a purpose that no human or event can rob from them? Towards that end, I march on.

I know what it's like to build a dream while having no

resources or prominent family name that can help. But I also know what it's like to have God Almighty by your side and to watch the flood waters part and to hear how one word from His mouth silences the most turbulent storms. This is God's story. I pray He will tell it through me to fill your heart with hope and to astound you with His greatness.

INSPIRE WOMEN WAS ESTABLISHED IN MAY OF 2003 beginning with zero in the bank, no office space and no infrastructure. God picked an emotional orphan from Hong Kong to lead the charge to inspire women across ethnicities and economic levels to connect their lives with God's purpose and to step into their divine appointments. In six month's time, Inspire Women produced a citywide conference and luncheon that reached nearly 4,000 women. Within a year and a half, Inspire Women invested over half a million dollars to inspire and to train women for God's purpose. Approximately 60% of our scholarship applicants come from backgrounds of abuse and see their training as giving them a chance to transform their pain into a positive ministry to those coming from similar backgrounds as their own. 40% are community and ministry leaders whose churches and families do not have the funds to train them for more effective ministry to their multi-ethnic communities.

In an unprecedented move by a donor towards a grassroots women's organization, Inspire Women received the first pledge into an endowment to ensure the perpetual existence of the organization as a gift to the city. The vision of Inspire Women is to invest in women who change the world with the power of God's Word. The organization is raising an endowment of $7.5 million to invest in the inspiration and training of women to help them to leave a legacy of eternal significance.

1

Just Trying to *Make It!*

Proverbs 13:12 reads, "Hope deferred makes the heart sick but a longing fulfilled is a tree of life." The problem with dreams is that they never die. Even when all hope for the fulfillment of a dream is gone, our heart secretly longs for the dream that refuses to be buried. How do you live with the events that robbed you of your childhood, your health, your loved ones? How do you restore the years the locusts have eaten? How do you make peace with a potential that is frustrated? How do you embrace a new future when your heart is tied to dreams in your past?

At Inspire Women, as we labor to help women to connect their lives with God's purpose, we speak in terms of "stepping into your divine appointment." We speak of an eternal God who has a timeline that stretches from yesterday, today, till a future forever. He was here long before we came on the scene and He will be here long after we are gone. In fact, we are but a breath in a mighty wind that is blowing from one end of the universe to the other. King David put it this way in Psalm 103:15-18, "As for man, his days are like grass, he flourishes like a flower of the field; the wind blows over it and it is gone, and its place remembers it no more. But from everlasting to everlasting the LORD's love is with those who fear him, and his righteousness with their children's children — with those who keep his covenant and remember to obey his precepts."

The vain attempt of fallen humanity is to mark our significance and to become consumed in our own stories. The fact is, all things were created for Him and by Him and my personal life only takes on significance when I lose my life in what God is doing. Did I always know this? Hardly. I was too busy reacting to what was going on around me and believing that my role in life was just to survive. The thought that I was here to make a statement for God never entered my mind. For that matter, I had no idea what statement God wanted to make. God was a power I cried out to in order to deliver me from harm. He represented goodness and purity but it never dawned on me that He had a dream of His own. To me, He existed to help MY dreams come true. In the midst of my ignorance, He was working. Before I was born, He knew me and He had a purpose for my life.

"NOTHING MY MOTHER PREDICTED FOR MY LIFE CAME TRUE"

MY MOTHER LOOKED AT MY HANDS ONE DAY AND tried to predict my future. She said my fingers belonged to that of a worker as compared to a Tai-Tai, a woman married to a rich man who spent her days shopping and playing mahjong. My mother did not think I possessed the fine lean fingers that carried a manicure well and with that, she predicted my future.

She also told me I was an unwanted pregnancy: I remember on my tenth birthday, no one said a word. When my mother found me lamenting at the end of the day because I received no gift, she went to a neighbor to borrow the money to shop for me. She returned in a most animated way bearing gift in hand. I remember vividly receiving an aluminum chicken painted in the most vibrant colors. It had a switch that when turned on, caused the chicken to cluck and to spin around in circles and to lay five plastic eggs, one after the other. When my father returned home, he was not happy with the acquisition. I had no idea then how tight money was. It broke my father's heart any time he could not afford to give to his children. I wish I had known this, but he struggled quietly. So, as a child, I interpreted his irritation as my fault. I was sorry I was a burden to the family.

When I read cards that said "God smiled the day you were born" I would think to myself, "No, He didn't. In fact, He must have wept." Against the bleak landscape of life, was the truth I had yet to discover. King David said in the book of Psalm 139:13-16, "For you created my inmost being; you knit me together in my mother's womb. I praise you because I am fearfully and wonderfully made; your works are wonderful, I know that full well. My frame was not hidden from you when I was made in the secret place. When I was woven together in the depths of the earth, your eyes saw my unformed body. All the days ordained for me were written in your book before one of them came to be."

Nothing my mother predicted for my life came true. She feared I would have a hard life. Instead I have a blessed life. I do not have a hard life but I have a hard working life. My life does not look like anything my mother would have imagined for me. All my life, she stressed the importance of financial independence. I chose not to live in her fears but willingly walked away from a corporate paycheck to choose to rest my financial provision in God's hands. I found peace in the fact that I was entrusted to my mother for a season but ultimately I was formed in her womb by God Almighty and He had a purpose for my life from now to eternity.

"I SEARCHED FOR A SAFE SANCTUARY IN WHICH TO HIDE..."

As I LOOK BACK ON MY FORMATIVE YEARS, I SEE God's hand in all the details of my life. It was as if He designed the perfect setting where I would grow to become what was needed for moments in His story. At the time, I felt I was in a pressure cooker that was about to explode. From the political unrest in my city, to the robberies and violence in my neighborhood, to the emotional outbursts between my mother and father as they struggled to make ends meet, I searched for a safe sanctuary in which to hide.

Although God protected me, He did not spare me. I would have preferred to disappear into a life of fairy tale and fantasy. But God allowed the suffering of the real world to enter my private world so that He could one day send me out in His name with His message of hope.

From the start, my feet were planted both in the world of the poor and the world of the affluent. When I reflect on God's design in where He planted me physically during the week and during weekends, I marvel at a God who was in control from the very beginning. My father was a tennis enthusiast and in spite of the tight finances, we were members of a country club where he spent every weekend playing tennis. I tagged along and played with the children of the club members, most of whom were British.

I did not realize we were from different socioeconomic levels. They probably did not realize this fact either considering my mother was a talented seamstress and made my sister and me designer looking clothes out of bargain fabric from the market. It never occurred to me that no one was ever invited to our home and that my mother was introducing me to a different world so that I could aspire to a more elegant lifestyle. At the time, I did not know I needed to be exposed to a different reality. In the same way, David the shepherd boy was brought into the royal courts of Saul because God knew that one day King David would need to know how to conduct himself in royal circles, God planted me among the affluent so I would not be intimidated to work with the rich.

My world during the week was not prim and proper as the country club environment. When I think of the physical structure of the three story apartment building I lived in, it represented a most unique stage for the cosmic play God was writing. Within that structure the complicated stories of the different tenants came alive.

Imagine standing with me at the entrance to the apartment building in which I spent my early childhood years. To the right of the entrance is a bar, advertised with bold flashing neon lights. To the left is a restaurant with a huge window displaying steamed dumplings. As you enter the building, you see a straight flight of concrete steps on the right. On the left is a three-foot area leading to a dead space behind the stairs where a hawker, his wife, his toddler and infant had created their home. This taught me from a young age how little we need when life is uncertain. As long as each member of the family is safe and goes to bed with a full stomach, all is well with the world. At the end of the day, what matters most are the people we shared our journey with and the hope we leave them along the way.

My routine coming from school was to ring the doorbell at the bottom of the stairs and to yell for my mother. She would then yell back if the coast was clear. This was my cue to run as fast as possible up the stairs before an assailant could trap me in the stairwell. My mother forced this ritual on us when my girlfriend was raped while com-

ing back from school. My mother's fear further intensi-
fied when a young thug chased her up the stairs. I remember her screaming for me to open the door. I remember
her banging on the door. I remember opening the door and
slamming it shut just before a strange pair of hands could
grab her.

Soon after, my father brought home a German
Shepherd thinking the dog would offer us protection. We
were surprised to come home one day to find that someone had broken into the apartment. It was the strangest
feeling to see my clothes scattered all over the bedroom
floor. The intruder took nothing. My parents said they
were just looking for cash. Where was the dog? He was
shut up by the intruder in a back room. That was the end
of trusting a dog for our protection. I felt insecure for several weeks. Someone had violated our personal space.

The morning after, as I walked to school I felt the eyes
of the vendors watching me. Were any of them involved?
Did anyone see anything? I knew no one would say a
word because the general feeling of those around me was
"Just mind your own business. You have enough problems of your own." My parents were the same way.

One evening during a thunderstorm, I heard a baby's
cry. I opened the door and found a newborn baby outside
our apartment door. It had just been delivered and the
umbilical cord was still visible. My mother told me that
someone who could not afford to feed the baby, left it, and
was watching to see if we would take the baby in. I wanted to take the baby. She told me I was an idealistic dream-

er. She called the police and they took the baby away. I never found out who the mother was and wondered, "Is she a vendor who watches me every morning when I go to school? Why did she leave the baby at our doorstep? Did she think I looked kind? Did I let her down?"

THERE IS NO PLACE FOR A PHILOSOPHER WHEN MONEY IS TIGHT

I did not know any of the tenants personally but I watched their lives. On the first floor, I discovered one of the apartments was filled with bunk beds. The only reason I knew of the apartment with the bunk beds was because I was passing by one day and someone had left the door open. This apartment belonged to the restaurant and it was packed with the kitchen boys and waiters. The apartment on the opposite side belonged to a tailor. I remember seeing rolls of fabric and a large cutting table.

I lived on the second floor. The neighbors above me were two prostitutes. I remember walking behind them as I came home from school one day. I was in my pure white uniform from the mission school. They were in mini skirts with their arms wrapped around the arms of the sailors from the navy. When I went home, I made a critical comment about their lives. My mother immediately corrected me. She scolded, "Don't judge! You have no idea what kind of situation the girls are in. Some have families in China they are supporting. They have no education. They are desperate and doing what they can to support their families. There are people in this city who are just trying to make it."

"Just trying to make it,"…those words ruled my life during my formative years. But deep inside, I always wondered if "making it" was all that life was about. Was the goal to move to bigger space, to cleaner space, to safer space, to more beautifully designed space? Do we keep moving up from neighborhood to neighborhood? And then what happens? I was always asking the question, "And then what?"

My mother called me a dreamer. I asked these life questions while she was mixing water with the eggs to stretch the evening meal. I had no idea what my father thought. He was so busy trying to make it that there was little time for conversation, at least not the kind of conversation I leaned towards. There is no place for a philosopher when money is tight. The only topics that made it to the table were questions about rent increase, ways to cut the budget, and what good deals were around the corner that could help us "make it." Then, as a distraction from the daily grind, my father escaped to play tennis every weekend and brought home the drama from his tennis friends.

Did I know that so and so ran off with so and so? I felt like I was living in two soap operas, one from the more affluent and one from the poor. Although their settings were different each group longed for the same thing – for life to be better just around the corner.

From my bedroom window, I could see another apartment building twenty-five feet from my building. Between our buildings was an alley where individual hawkers set up. One was a cobbler who encircled his space with a piece of fabric like an old fashioned shower curtain. During the evenings, he shut the curtains and made his vendor space his sleeping space. One day, I noticed he was gone. My mother simply said he was a drug addict and overdosed. That was the end of the conversation. People leaped off buildings, people died, and life went on. In the same way that Moses was connected to the struggles of the Hebrew slaves who toiled in the hot sun, God put me where I could feel the pain of the people around me. Moses did not go to lead the people to the Promise Land because it was his idea. He felt totally inadequate to respond to the needs of the people. Moses went because God in His mercy raised up a servant in His name. Like this great Bible story, I did not establish Inspire Women because I thought it was such a good idea. It was birthed by God who then put His baby in my arms.

Across the alley, I could see that in one of the apartments, young girls came in every day to assemble plastic flowers. My mother would always warn me that if I didn't study hard enough to get a seat in school, I would end up in a factory assembling flowers. I found out very early that privileges were earned. Life was not handed to me on a silver platter. I had to pass a citywide exam to keep my seat in school. Students were screened out in sixth grade. I could continue in school into seventh grade only if I did well enough on the exam.

I remember the morning when the local newspaper printed all the identity numbers of the students who passed the test. I tried to pretend I was asleep because I was afraid to wake up and face reality. I heard the crinkle of the newspaper as my father searched for my number. He slammed the newspaper on the table and said, "She didn't make it." My stomach cramped. Was I heading for the factory? What exactly was my future? My mother immediately said, "Let me look." The newspaper crinkled again. I began to sweat under my blankets. Then I heard my mother say, "You silly man, here it is. She made it. Here is her number." In that split second, life took a turn but it could have gone the other way. What does it mean when one door shuts and one door opens?

My mother used to speak of luck and chance. But the concept of chance does not exist in the Bible. God is the Master Planner. All things were created by Him and for Him.

From the windows on the adjacent side of our apartment, I could see a row of apartment buildings two hundred feet from our building. In between us was an open market. The vendors came from the New Territories, the country part of the city. It was amazing to go to the New Territories. I remember going through a tunnel carved through the Lion Rock Mountain. On one side of the mountain was the city life of Hong Kong. On the other side of the mountain were farmland and the country. I didn't need an alarm clock at home. I knew it was morning when the trucks started rolling in and the hawkers and farmers from the New Territories began unloading their goods. Each had a pre-assigned booth where they displayed their products. They sold fresh eggs and fruit. They sold fresh vegetables. They brought chickens by the basketfuls.

Before I went to full time school, my mornings consisted of tagging along with my mother as she went to market. Eating food that is fresh was considered critical to one's health. I had never seen fish in a can till I arrived in the United States. Although there were some grocery stores in my city, my mother shopped in the open market and not a grocery store. The very thought of frozen food was foreign to me. My mother went to market once in the morning and once in the afternoon. We knew the chicken was fresh because we watched the chicken farmer slaughter the chicken right in front of us. The eggs were piled up like a mountain. To this day, I'm not sure why the egg vendor takes each egg and places it up against a lamp before putting it in our shopping bag. My mother said he was checking to make sure the yolk was whole and that it was not forming a chick.

In the open marketplace there were stray dogs and puppies running around. They stayed near the market to eat the garbage. There were stray cats and kittens. Vendors would holler out their bargains. Buyers would bicker over the price and argued why the price should be lower. The whole environment around me was filled with people and animals trying to "make it". I wonder if the practice of bargaining comes from countries where people are trying to "make it".

I remember when I was relocated to Brussels, Belgium, I wanted to bargain for the rent. My American friends were appalled. They would never have thought to bargain for a lower price. To their surprise, the Belgian landlord took my bargain offer. When the word got around, others were encouraged to do the same. I learned that in the American culture, success was often the measuring stick of whether something was the right thing to do. No matter how great the criticism, the bottom line question was, "Did it work?" If it worked, then it was the right thing to do.

MY CHILDHOOD MOMENTS SERVED AS COMIC RELIEF

IN SPITE OF THE POLITICAL TENSION, THE CULTURAL differences and the social problems in my city, deep inside I was still just an adolescent trying to make sense of the world. When I reflect on the childhood moments of my youth, I realize they served as comic relief. Moreover, they show me that in spite of what I witnessed or wrestled with, deep inside I was just a kid. Oh how I marvel at a God who had His hands of protection on me the entire time. Even though He allowed hardships in my life, they were entrusted to me for the work He planned for me in the future. He was not afraid to give me some crosses to

bear because He was sure His strength would be suffi-
cient. God definitely believed in His power in me more
than I did. He was not in a hurry. He did not panic when
I was confused. He knew that, in time, He would weave
together all the moments of my life to make a difference
for Him in a fallen world.

When I reflect on some of the lighter moments in my
childhood memories, I feel more normal. At least there
were incidents I can recall that remind me I was once a
child who did not always feel the weight of the world on
my shoulders. The long corridor in my Hong Kong apartment led to a kitchen at the back. Outside the kitchen was
a small veranda. From the veranda I could see the apartment building across the alley. Below me was a patio.
Only the apartments on ground level had patios.

There were no potted plants or patio furniture so typical for patios in this country. The patio immediately
below me belonged to the apartment with all the kitchen
boys and waiters. In this patio were old chairs and tables
from the restaurants. It looked like someone just took a
dump truck and unloaded all the excess furniture. For
many who are trying to make ends meet, space served no
purpose unless it helped you make a living. The patio was
used as a storage space. The idea of making a space pretty was a luxury many could not afford.

The furniture made for a perfect hiding place for some
wild cats. My mother called them wild because they were
born in the street and survived on garbage. They never
experienced the touch from human hands. If you tried to

approach them, they would attack you. One of the cats had kittens, and before long, they would come out of hiding and play on the furniture. I had my eye on one particular kitten that had blue eyes with the prettiest black and white fur. I came up with a most ingenious idea to trap a Hong Kong cat. I dangled down a brown paper sack filled with a chicken leg from dinner the night before. As soon as the kitten crawled into the bag, I snatched the bag up and captured the kitten.

My adrenaline started flowing as I felt the weight in the brown paper bag. I started reeling in my catch when, all of a sudden, I heard the growl of the mama cat. On either side of the patio was a chain link fence that almost reached to the second level. To my surprise, the mother cat started climbing up the fence and she was heading right towards me. Our eyes met and it scared me as I looked into the angriest pair of amber eyes. By this time, the brown bag was only two feet from my grasp but I let go of the string and the bag dropped to the ground. The kitten jumped out of the bag and the mother cat leaped off the fence. Whoa, that was a close call! I could feel my heart pounding.

I decided after that to go for a safer pet. I persuaded my mother to rescue a frog from the marketplace who was destined to be someone's dinner that evening. I took it for walks by putting it on a leash made of straw reed. To make it walk, I jumped on the ground right behind it which caused the frog to hop forward. It took a long time to go from point A to point B as we hopped along. The sad thing was I could not figure out how to feed the frog. I tried killing a fly and putting it on the frog's lip. Mother said that frogs only ate flies that were alive. Within a week the frog died. I was heartbroken that I did not figure out a way to save it.

The next pet I acquired was a goose I won from a school bazaar. I played one of those games where I was asked to toss three rings around a flock of geese. If one of the rings ended up around the goose's neck, I won the goose. So, I found myself walking home with a big brown box with a goose in it. The cardboard box was taped at the top but on my way home, the goose pushed the tape loose. So, out came this head that started looking this way and that while I walked. I must have been quite a sight to behold. As soon as I got home, my mother said, "Let's eat the goose for dinner." The thought horrified me. How could she even suggest such an idea? Once again, I attempted to have a pet that was not created to be pet material. The goose would not eat. It went from being a plump goose to being skin and bones. My mother said, "We might as well eat it before it dies." Reluctantly, I consented to allowing the goose to be slaughtered. When dinner was served, all I remembered was staring at my pet on the dining table. The whole meal time, my mother complained about how the goose used to have a lot of meat on it, but now it was just skin and bones.

WHAT ARE YOU DOING
WITH YOUR LIFE?

MY FATHER MUST HAVE FELT SORRY FOR ME. HE
told me he had a friend who loved dogs and he would ask
a favor of him to find us a pet. His friend was a captain on
a ship. The next I knew, I was awaiting a pet from Japan.
I'm not sure why my father picked Japan as the place
from which my pet would set sail, but the thought sounded very exquisite.

I came home from school one day to find the most darling fluffy white Maltese. Was that a dog from Japan, I
wondered? The dog was actually from Malta, but was
born in Tokyo, Japan. My father said it was the Captain's
personal dog. Ours had gotten ill on the boat and the captain's wife did not want him to hand us a sick dog, so he
gave us his own. My father said we could never have
afforded such a pet. So here I was in a neighborhood
where people were trying to make it, walking around with
a Maltese.

While everyone relegated it to the title of dog, I saw it
as a champion and the star performer during our dinner
parties and social visits. This little Maltese dog became
my best friend. Her name was Cappy. I don't know why I
would not allow Cappy to be just a normal dog. Instead, I
assessed Cappy to possess superior intelligence. So surely, Cappy was destined to do things that surpassed the
ordinary hound.

I taught Cappy how to count. I put up one finger and barked for her. She got the idea. As soon as I put up one finger, Cappy would bark once. Then I put up two fingers and barked twice. Once again, Cappy got the idea. So she barked twice. This went on till I had all five fingers raised in one hand and two fingers on the other hand. Cappy made it up to seven and then she would lose count and just barked nonstop continuously. I figured I had reached Cappy's potential. Her limit was seven. If I pushed her further, she would unravel mentally. So I stopped at seven. I don't know how many other children assess the potential of their pet before they design a training plan. Did God give me a passion to develop the potential in His creation from way back then in my childhood? I'm not sure if Cappy considered herself lucky. She would probably have preferred to lie around and to grow fat. But I didn't give her that choice.

I haven't changed much since those days of years ago. Nowadays, when I am around people, my mind immediately wants to ask, "What are you doing with your life? Where are you compared to the potential God has put within you?" Is it a coincidence or divine providence that Inspire Women exists to help women to discover God's calling for their lives and to train them to step into their divine purpose?

GOD TEACHES US WHAT WE NEED FOR THE WORK HE HAS DESIGNED FOR US

BACK IN HONG KONG, FROM THE VERANDA OUTSIDE the kitchen, my mother would take her chopping board and chop the beef into hamburger meat or peel the shells from the shrimp that went into the wontons she was making. I recall the neighbor next to us coming out to the veranda adjacent to ours and she and my mother would start speaking in Mandarin. Although I understood what they were saying I was not familiar enough with their dialect to speak it. The main languages I was brought up with in Hong Kong were British or Cantonese.

The tenant in the building across the alley from us came out to her veranda and was slaughtering a chicken. This tenant was dressed in her native attire. She was clearly not from our culture. I could tell that my mother and our neighbor started saying words beneath their breath. They were both agreeing to the total inappropriateness of how the tenant across the street slaughtered her chicken. Apparently, there was a right way and a wrong way. There was a merciful way and a cruel way. My mother and our neighbor were convinced that the Chinese were more merciful. So, on and on, the conversation went.

Over and over again, I witnessed incidents that reminded me of the many unspoken rules in different cultures. I'm not even sure how those rules came about, but

I know that if you violate them, you are immediately excluded as an outsider. What was most fascinating was how the people in local communities were very emotional about their unspoken rules and customs.

As I grew up amidst the diversity in different cultures, I did not realize then that God was preparing me to work cross culturally. More than that, my efforts would cross economic levels and different social levels. Different groups have their own unspoken rules which they see as law. It's safer to stay within your own groups but when you venture out, you may inadvertently step on some toes out of ignorance. However, whenever I have offended without meaning to because I was ignorant about a certain protocol, God shows me that He never said His calling would be easy. Would I shrivel up on the inside and wish the ground would just swallow me up? Or would I have the humility to ask for forgiveness and to do what it takes to build bridges? Did I learn this from the discussion over the right way to kill a chicken? It's amazing to me how creative God is to teach us what we need for the work He has designed for us. I cannot allow myself to be defensive because I know the reason why cultures have unspoken customs and rules: They provide safety and familiarity.

In the East, it is considered a great honor when someone shows up in person to extend an invitation. In fact, the higher the rank of the person who shows up, the greater is the honor. I learned that in America, it might be construed as pushy to show up in person. Being someone whom God has transplanted from culture to culture, I find myself learning the rules frantically as I travel from one subgroup to another. Sometimes, I get discouraged by the rules of culture because it seems that we could move so much faster to accomplish what's important if we didn't have to figure out all the different protocols of each subgroup. I praise God for those who have shown me grace when I inadvertently offended, and I grieve over those who have allowed cultural differences to divide. But even in this, God teaches me that cultural tension results when one party feels dominant and demands the world to see life their way. God teaches me that unity and peace in a community is only possible when we humble ourselves before God and before each other. God teaches me that any time you try to reach outside of your group, you risk making mistakes. The question is, "Will you still take the risk? Will you keep trying because building bridges is worth more to you than building walls that separate a community?"

As Inspire Women works to affirm the potential in women across ethnicities and economic levels, we are working to inspire a vision that transcends individual cultures. There is a goal that is greater than one individual's preferences. There is a mission with eternal consequences that can be more fully realized when we affirm the gift in each person to offer God's hope, and overlook the styles that govern how we do things. The alternative is to allow ourselves to be offended by things that don't matter, to put up more walls that divide, to find more reasons why we can't get along, and to waste emotional energy on disagreements that have no eternal significance.

THOUGH MY FATHER AND MOTHER FORSAKE ME

WHEN MY MOTHER FINISHED HER WORK ON THE veranda, I lingered to watch the activity in the alley. I saw a mother drag a little girl who looked to be around five years of age. From what the mother was saying, I gathered she was one of the cooks in the kitchen. She had asked her daughter to watch her two-year-old brother. The little girl ran off to play and the mother was disciplining her for being irresponsible.

The kitchen boys gathered around to watch the scene. They were smoking cigarettes, jeering and taking bets on what would happen next. The mother used her strength to force the little girl to the ground. She tied her hands behind her back with kitchen twine. She tied her feet up, she took what looked like the end of a broom stick and she struck the girl on the leg. In between the blows, she lectured her on why she was being punished and asked her if she would ever dare to leave her brother unattended again. The little girl begged for mercy and told her mother over and over again that she would never disobey her again. The mother waited a few seconds and struck her again. All the while, the kitchen boys shouted and cheered. The girl's face was towards the concrete.

She turned her head and in one split second, her eyes

gazed towards the veranda where I stood. I saw her tears smeared across her face. I ducked down on the veranda because I didn't want her to know that I had seen her shame. I could hardly bear thinking of how she was feeling.

What does it feel like to be ridiculed by your own mother in front of the crowds? What does it feel like to be victimized while everyone is watching and no one will intervene to deliver you?

I ran inside to tell my mother and begged her to do something. She told me the city was filled with people with many problems. Moreover, we had problems of our own and you never knew if someone had relatives who were members of a gang. If we intervened, we could be the target of someone's vengeance. My mother would not call the police. She said, "The police are too busy with the drug smugglers and the big problems. This is a local problem. They won't care what a mother is doing to her own child."

The fact struck me that the inner circle can be the cruelest. I learned that the deepest scars are those made by the one we trusted as our friend. King David said in Psalm 55:12-14, "If an enemy were insulting me, I could endure it; if a foe were raising himself against me, I could hide from him. But it is you, a man like myself, my companion, my close friend, with whom I once enjoyed sweet fellowship as we walked with the throng at the house of God." I did not know, as I do now, that King David also learned and shared with us in Psalm 27:10, "Though my father and mother forsake me, the LORD will receive me." From heaven's throne, God was watching. I cried out, "God, why don't you do something?" Nothing changed. I thought God didn't care.

Today, I realize God was doing something. He was preparing me to go in His name. For all those who never had God's intended parent figure, for all those whose spirit was crushed by those who abused their power, for all those who could not find an advocate to invest in their ability to make a difference, for all those who could not find their voice in the shadow of an overbearing parent, would Inspire Women come along side and help them discover their God-designed purpose and train them for their calling? Would we invest in the potential of women of all ethnicities and release the full potential of all God's daughters to find significance in an eternal legacy?

I went back out to the veranda. By this time, it looked like the action was over. The mother had gone back to work and so had the kitchen boys. The little girl lay alone on the grime-filled concrete with her face to the ground. She looked like she wished the ground would just open up and swallow her. Her hands were still tied behind her back. One of the kitchen boys came out with a pen knife and cut her loose. She still laid there on the ground, afraid to move. I decided at that moment that there was something very wrong with those who used their strength to destroy the spirit of the weak. We were never meant to use our power to lord it over others. We were entrusted with power in order to bless and not to abuse.

WILL SOMEONE BELIEVE IN ME?

I WOKE UP THE NEXT DAY TRYING TO ACT NORMAL, BUT I wasn't sure what normal was anymore. I ran down the stairs on my way to school and ran right into a man from the country club. He looked as shocked as I did. It was seven in the morning and he was just leaving the bar. I could see the question in his eyes. He was looking at me and wondering, "What in the world are you doing in this part of the neighborhood?" I was looking at him and wondering, "Aren't you a married man? What are you doing coming out of a bar at seven in the morning?" Neither of us spoke a word. I turned abruptly and started walking away. He turned abruptly and went the other way. The next weekend, I saw him at the country club; neither of us looked at each other. When we spoke, things were as "normal." I learned that "normal" is a façade. Things are not always what they seem. However, many times we let things "be" because revealing the truth would require making changes. Sometimes, we live a lie because it feels easier and less complicated than dealing with the truth.

While we live our lies, the potential that God puts in us goes undeveloped. What was God's original design for those women who were living as prostitutes above my apartment? What was God's dream for that little girl who was abused in the alley? Nearly sixty percent percent of the women who come to Inspire Women asking us to train them for ministry come from backgrounds of abuse. They are not asking to be trained so they can get a job. They are embracing the cross God entrusted them to carry. When I hear their stories, I am reminded of that little girl in the alley. They are crying out, "Will someone believe in me? Will someone help me to make sense of the pain and to find a divine purpose that will reach back in mercy to those who come from similar backgrounds as my own?" In their requests, I hear their courage to return to the battleground from which they barely survived in order to bring the power of God's healing and hope to those who are suffering from the kind of abuse and rejection they personally experienced. In the same way that we would never send our military into enemy territory without the proper ammunition, God longs for His spiritual warriors to enter His service with the proper training.

About forty percent of those who apply for scholarship funding from Inspire Women are community and ministry leaders whose families and churches do not have the funds to train them for more effective ministry. They are not asking for funds so they can make more money in a career. They just want to help people.

How much potential has been lost because we did not empower those who were willing to serve? When God walked on earth, He was our example. He spoke words of blessing. When He touched someone, His hand brought healing. He offered hope to those who were in despair. He overturned the tables of the vendors who were cheating in the temple. He did not tolerate hypocrisy. He defined "normal" as people who were filled with His satisfaction and living His purpose. "Normal", in God's eyes was meant to be a reservoir that overflows with never-ending satisfaction. "Normal" was not just trying to "make it" or filling our lives with distractions to hide the true emptiness in our soul. Can you imagine how the world would be if we all understood the world God intended?

Our purpose, then, is to bring restoration to what fallen humanity has destroyed. We are on a rescue mission to look at things with the eyes of our heavenly Father and to go in His name, to leave His character and purpose wherever we go. Towards that end of inspiring and mobilizing women to step into their divine calling, Inspire Women marches.

Each of us is the culmination of all our experiences. We have a personal history that is ours alone. We can choose to keep our stories as our own crosses to bear and consume ourselves in nursing our wounds or we can give our stories to God. When we give up our stories, God takes our uniqueness and walks us into a place in history where our personal story dovetails into the story of what God is doing in a community. We become His custom-tailored servant He has prepared to step into our moments in His story.

In the story of Jeremiah, God said in Jeremiah 1:5, "Before I formed you in the womb I knew you, before you were born I set you apart; I appointed you as a prophet to the nations." In our story, our moment of discovery is when we realize we do not choose the part we play in God's story. He is the one who has chosen. Every cross He entrusted to us takes on meaning when we offer our suffering to Him. Every heartache conforms us to His heart of mercy and compassion. Is it only when we ask, "How can God tell His story through mine?" that we start reading from a divine script. It is only then that we discover that all experiences will culminate towards a grand finale that God is writing. It is then that we are astounded in a God who would even look our way. We are in awe and humbled that the God of the Universe has worked out all things for good to give us a part in a story of great significance.

2

The Truth Behind the Charade

"SING!" MY MOTHER SAID AS SHE PULLED ME OUT OF MY chair while walking by me on her way to the kitchen. "You girls are young. You should be full of life!" she chided as my sister buried her head in a novel and I was busy writing a poem about life.

MY MOTHER'S ONLY TANGIBLE HOPE FOR A BETTER FUTURE

I ALWAYS THOUGHT MY MOTHER SHOULD HAVE BEEN A star. I found out she once tried out for a part in a musical. Perhaps because she never made it in the theater, she made our home her stage. She went from peeling shrimp intensely or spending hours on a sewing project to dancing through the house with a song in her heart. Despite all the singing on the outside, there were times when I would catch my mother in deep reflection. It was as if she slipped into a world of her own. Or perhaps it was a past world from which she came from, with secrets and heartaches she never revealed.

When my older son Robbie was eight years old, he asked me a question that normally does not come out of a child's mouth. He said, "Mom, when you look back at your past, what do you wish you could do all over again?" His question reminded me of those moments when I saw the regret on my mother's face. What heartache was she hiding? Dare I ask and open the floodgates of her sorrow?

When my mother had her head in a sewing project, she spent hours on her creation. The way she started sewing was so typical of how she began any project. If you told her she couldn't do something it became her challenge to prove you wrong. Once there was a dress that she admired in a store window. She tried to convince the store vendor to sell it to her for a price she could afford. The vendor told her she was ridiculous and ridiculed her for suggesting such an absurd price. The next day, she saw the same fabric in the marketplace. So she bought it, found an old sewing machine and waltzed by the front window of the store to get a better look at the dress. Afterwards, she went home and figured out on her own how to cut out the pattern pieces and to sew the exact dress she saw in the shop window. The most wonderful moment of all came when she wore the dress to that store and paraded it in front of the store vendor who would not sell her the dress for the price she offered. So much for telling my mother she could not have what she wanted. Her sewing success, also gave her the capability to portray an image to the public that was contrary to our real economic level.

As I recall my mother's natural personality to overcome the odds that were against her, I now realize her utter frustration when her life was controlled by powers she could not influence. I remember seeing my mother in tears for a prolonged time when her father died. She wanted to return to China for the funeral but did not have the funds. Then there was the risk that if she went into mainland China, would there be a problem in leaving and returning to Hong Kong? What would happen to her daughters if she were stuck in China? Have you ever wanted something in your life but felt utterly helpless to reach for it? I came home to find her dressed in black. For the next thirty days, I would catch her holding the picture frame which carried her father's photograph, with tears rolling down her face. That month, there was no laughter in the house.

Sometimes I wonder if the reason that education was such a priority in my home was because it was my mother's only tangible hope for a better future. She never went past a third-grade education. No one could ever tell though because she encompassed a spirit that lifted her above the crowds. She also understood people and their motives. On top of that, she had a pure heart that wanted what was right. She believed in the God who sent His one and only son to die for our sins. Such a God has proven His love. Such a God who raised Jesus from the dead surely has the power to intervene in our lives if He chooses. When you combine her passion with her purity, with her creativity, with her belief in a good God, you find a dynamo package. She exuberated confidence to all those around us that victory was around the corner.

My mother was the one who taught my sister and me how to write and how to make speeches. She would read my materials and say, "Please have mercy on your teachers. Everyone begins their essay that way. Be different!" When my sister was in a speech competition, my mother watched the preliminaries and was sure to point out to my sister the presentation she loved the most. It was from a student who did not just memorize her speech but dramatized her speech. She began with the words, "Noise, noise, everywhere" as she gestured with her hands and walked intentionally in a choreographed pattern. What a novel idea compared to the many who began with, "Today I would like to talk to you about the noise level in our city." My sister told my mother she wasn't about to make a fool of herself. My mother said, "In that case, you won't win." And that was the end of that conversation.

It was with passion that my mother drilled us in our academics. When my sister could not remember the words of a poem she had to memorize, my mother flapped her arms like a bird's wings and cried, "The words are 'Fly, fly, fly like a bird." What my mother did not realize was that there was a pencil on the bed on which she was sitting. So when her arms flapped down onto the bed, the end of the pencil went into her palm. That was the end of the flapping bird. My mother had to rush to the emergency room to get the lead taken out of her hands. She left the house warning my sister to keep studying and to know the words by the time she returned.

HOW MANY DREAMS CAN WE BURY BEFORE THE ASHES SUFFOCATE US?

I'm not sure at what point my mother regretted her own lack of formal education. All I remember is coming home one day and seeing her pouring over homework. She was determined to get her high school diploma. I wish I had been more sensitive to her dreams. I remember how she pleaded with my sister and me to help around the house so she could study. I had no idea then how hard it was for my mother to study as an adult to try to restore the years she never had in her youth.

How do you believe in your own potential when no one else believes in you? How do you bless the child within you that continues to seek expression and freedom when you have children of your own to raise? In the midst of your duties, how do you focus on books and academics? Meanwhile, there was always the pressure that your dream was costing the family financially because when discretionary income is low, a woman's dream is often the last to be funded. All I know is that one day, the books just disappeared. Did she ever reach her goal or did she simply give up? She was never one to give up but she was prone to weighing the choices. If it was between benefiting herself or benefiting her children, she would lay down her dreams for her children. Was it my dream to develop something in me that redirected the family's finances and influenced her to give up what she wanted for herself?

How many dreams can we bury before the ashes suffocate us? I never sensed any resentment from my mother, only sorrow. There were so many things in life my mother felt powerless to change. She had dreams which were dependent on someone else's decisions. She was a visionary leader and saw opportunities for my father in business. Against her personality to take a chance for a better future was his personality to do what was safe to protect the future. There were times when I sensed her total frustration. Because she did not have a formal education, she could not step into the opportunities that she saw. It was only after she died that my father went into the business venture my mother had begged him to get into for years. He became more prosperous than ever. She never enjoyed the fruit of his success.

I wonder if my mother pushed her children to rise above the crowd because she sensed there is greatness in all of us that life tries to destroy. Perhaps she focused her attention on us because at least we were still moldable. She had a passion for what was right and for what was good. The fight in her rose when she sensed that darkness was trying to snuff out the light. But she never jumped into the battle prematurely because she understood the value of right timing. Sometimes the best way to fight is to first get prepared. Sometimes the only way to win is to wait. Until you are strong enough, entering a fight too soon is a sure way to get yourself killed. At the end of the day, all you would be left with are your good intentions.

My mother watched and she waited. Her hope rested in the future of her children.

To answer my son's question on what I would do if I had the chance to live parts of my life all over again, I would say, "If I had to do it all over again, I would be a more sensitive listener of the dreams and heartaches of those around me."

THE FAÇADE BREAKS DOWN BEHIND CLOSED DOORS!

I**T'S HARD TO TRUST SOMEONE WHO HAS NO ROOTS.** During my childhood, Hong Kong was filled with so many refugees that trust or the lack of it shaped our relationships. Where did they come from? What kind of family did they have? What were they searching for? It seemed that everyone was trying to get ahead and few had the time or resources to help another.

My mother chatted with the neighbor on the veranda while she was preparing the evening meal, but that was the extent of their interaction. No one in my apartment building ever came over to our house except for one little girl I played with while growing up. Later on, her parents moved to a better neighborhood. We said we would keep in touch but over time, I never saw her again. People kept to themselves. Few were interested in investing in the community because they had enough trouble supporting their own families. Though I didn't know the tenants well,

I knew about them because of their proximity. There were times I wished I knew less.

From the living room area in my apartment was a fifteen foot corridor that led to the kitchen. Along the walls of the corridor were windows. I could look out those windows and see right into the living space of our neighbor. So much for privacy!

One afternoon, I was passing through the corridor when I heard an argument taking place. I could tell from where the shouts came from that it was from the apartment of the prostitutes. A man's voice said roughly, "You are from the gutters! Without me, you would have no roof over your head. You would be in the streets." Then I heard a lot of wailing. It sounded like he was leaving. It sounded like she was holding on to him. Then, there was a door that slammed and footsteps going down the stairs. Then I heard more wailing. Did she want him to stay? Why did she want him to stay? Was it love or was it desperation? My mother told me that with each tenant comes a deep history of heartaches and struggles.

I witnessed a similar wailing in a totally different economic setting. One of my father's contacts moved his business to Hong Kong. He, his wife and children became part of my family's life. I called them my aunt and uncle. I noticed that their living space was ten times bigger than ours. They had maids and chauffeurs. One of the seasonal fruits in our city was lychees. When they were in season, my mother rejoiced when we could purchase a dozen to share with the four in our family. I noticed my aunt bought lychees by the basketfuls. In fact, tubful might be a better word because the baskets were two feet wide and two feet deep. Through my aunt's relationships, I was exposed to the lifestyle of the wealthy. Parties took on a dimension beyond anything I had ever seen. I remember a wedding with a guest list of 2500 people. The parents had a personal chauffeur but they also had a chauffeur for the children. The logic was, you needed one chauffeur to wait for you while you are shopping and you needed another to take the children to their many activities. Money seemed to solve many problems including drawing ministers of God's Word to the house who would pray for your blessing in exchange for a check.

In spite of the financial extravagance, the façade breaks down behind closed doors. A wailing came from my aunt as she wrapped her hands around my uncle's ankles while he was storming out of the house. She was being dragged on the ground behind him as he shouted at her to let him go. I was in the upstairs of their residence when this scene took place on the lower level. Perhaps they were not aware that I was visiting with the kids.

I found out later that my uncle was involved with someone else's wife. He then involved my aunt with that woman's husband. This wife swapping had been going on behind the scenes while they portrayed to the public the image of a happy family. My aunt wanted to stop the wife swapping and my uncle was outraged. He was walking out and she was clinging on to his ankles. He finally kicked her loose and totally ignored the wailing and the pleading. He didn't have time for theatrics. He had to go and close a deal that would generate millions of dollars. He had all the financial power and as far as he was concerned, he ruled the world. I learned that whether in the poorest of neighborhood or in the wealthiest ones, the outcome is the same. When you are desperate for love from someone who feels they have all the power, you compromise your dignity.

When someone says, "I need you to love me," some people treat these words with great tenderness; however, there are those who treat such information with arrogance. When they know you need them, they will use your vulnerability against you. They totally missed the fact that any power they have was entrusted to them for God's purpose. God did not entrust them with power or influence in order to abuse and to lord it over others but to be a blessing and to show mercy. Jesus said to His disciples in Mark 10:42-45, "You know that those who are regarded as rulers of the Gentiles lord it over them, and their high officials exercise authority over them. Not so with you. Instead, whoever wants to become great among you must be your servant, and whoever wants to be first must be slave of all. For even the Son of Man did not come to be served, but to serve, and to give his life as a ransom for many."

MY ONLY HOPE WAS IN A GREATER POWER

I HURRIED TO PUT ON MY STARK WHITE UNIFORM FROM the mission school. I had a royal blue tie and a royal blue belt. I wore white socks and black shoes. As I left the building, one could hardly have imagined that I came from a world filled with so much drama. Before I left, my mother reminded me not to loiter. There were major uprisings in the city and the papers reported that the communists considered religion to be the opium of the people. There was warning of bombs being left at the gates of Christian schools. The night before, there was a curfew in the city. Everyone had to be off the streets by 7 p.m. As soon as the school bell rang, I ran home for fear that I would be caught in the streets. It appeared that my neighbor's son was not as vigilant because the next morning as I was going down the stairs on my way to school, he was coming home. I tried not to look at him because I could tell that he had been caught. His head had been shaven by the police as a way to visibly mark him as one who broke the curfew laws. I shuddered to think of being marked so visibly. I also could not relate to his wanting to be in the streets after curfew hours. I was scared to death of the crowds. They felt like some kind of vortex that draws in innocent bystanders. Before you know it, you're involved in some frenzied activity that destroys everything in its path. Anger has a way of escalating and I did not want to be anywhere near an angry mob. While my neighbor's son ventured into the streets, I was hiding in my bed. The world felt very small because danger was just outside my door. Isn't there somewhere in the world I could hide where I could find a safe sanctuary?

During the days of the curfew, as the clock ticked into the curfew hours, the streets grew quieter and quieter, but I knew it was an artificial silence. The silence was often broken by some flying object that smashed through a shop window. Then as if someone crashed open a gate that was pushing back a stampede, the mobs were unleashed to run down the streets while destroying anything in their path. There is something very eerie in the sound of the mob. Their voice begins in the distance and descends on you like a tidal wave. As they ran past my apartment, I could hear the distinct sound of army boots as the British army and the Hong Kong police chased in hot pursuit. The sound of tear gas bombs exploded and just as quickly as the mob erupted from the silence, the streets became silent once again.

As I laid there in my bed, I was trembling and sweating under my blankets. Then timidly, I peeked from under my blankets and my eyes looked through my bedroom window towards the sky. I was taken aback by the many stars that shone down on our city. How could there be such beauty in the midst of the darkness? The contrast intrigued me. Was there truly hope we can reach out to when the darkness feels overwhelming? Then out of a child's mouth came this prayer, "God, if you can see me, if you can find me among the millions in my city, please help me reach the free land of America." I didn't know much about America except for the television shows "Father Knows Best" and "Leave it to Beaver." My image of America was a land of peace and abundance. Little did I know that no matter what the country or culture or economic level, people around the world cannot escape from the losses in life. Sooner or later, we find our common bond in our struggles and heartaches.

In addition to the battles that were going on in the streets, I felt the crossfire of the battles that were going on within the four walls of the home in which I lived. Money has a way to bring out the worse in us. I remember my father's disappointment when he did not get the promotion he needed. He worked for a Dutch company and no matter how hard he worked; he was bypassed by a Dutch employee. My mother would say, "Don't worry. Work harder. Try again next year." The next year came and again my father did not receive what he had hoped for. I remember a tear rolling down his face. There were times when my mother was sympathetic, but I also saw times when her frustration in not reaching her dreams for our family made her accuse and criticize my father. I knew the boiling point had been reached when words started flaring. I don't remember the exact conversations but I remember the intensity in which they were spoken. I saw the power of words to destroy the human spirit. "You will amount to nothing!" is a declaration that is not easily forgotten. My sister and I would cling to each other and cry. We felt so helpless to stop the war that was going on in our own household. One day, I said to my sister, "Do you think they would stop fighting if I died or something?" We came up with the idea that I should pretend to faint. So as I sat at the edge of my bed, I simply toppled over and fell on the floor. My sister stepped into my parent's crossfire to make the statement, "I think Anita fainted or something." The battle stopped for a little while. My father carried me to the bed. My mother brought a wet cloth to wipe my face. They asked how I was feeling. As soon as I opened my eyes, they blamed each other for causing pain for the children. Then they went right back into their arguments. My sister looked at me and said, "Well, that didn't work."

At the time, I didn't understand what the quarrels were about. But now, I realize that when you hold dreams in your heart and you think someone is keeping you from your destiny, they somehow turn into your enemy. I think the deceit we live with is to believe that someone could possibly thwart God's dreams for our lives. I wish I knew God's truth then, but I did not. Therefore, I did not have the counsel from His Word to instruct my parents. I have learned since then that all things were created for God and by God. The challenge, therefore, is to ask, "What dream is God dreaming for my family, my community, and for the world? How can I respond to the challenges in life in a way to advance His purpose on earth?" If my parents had known this, they would have known that our challenges were but an opportunity for God to showcase His power; our need to persevere made the victory even grander; our successes only find value when they advance the story He wants to tell.

After the quarrels, my mother often sat silently by herself. I would see tears rolling down her cheeks. I was so afraid that one day, she would just run away. I told her if she ever thought of leaving, "Please take me with you!" She answered, "I can't support you. At least your father can feed you." I tried to appeal to my father to help my mother feel better. But I could tell that something in his spirit had died as well. No one wins when we allow our words to kill each other. Some days going to school was my way to escape from the battles in my home and the battles in my city. All the while, I lived with the fear of returning home one day to find that my mother would no longer be there.

Ever with me was my mother's warning about bombs being left at the gates of Christian schools. So, when I arrived at the school gate, I ran as fast as I could, thinking that perhaps if I ran, I might miss the shrapnel in case a bomb went off. As soon as I entered the gates of my Christian school, I stepped into another totally different world.

I began each morning in the school chapel. Often, no other students would be there except me. I sneaked in quietly after the nuns sang their final hymn. While they exited to their various responsibilities, I found a corner of the chapel and sat there quietly. I opened a hymn book and meditated on the life of Jesus. At the front of the chapel was a twenty-foot cross with a life sized Jesus hanging on it. I would look at the crown of thorns on his head. I would study the nails and the artist's rendering of the blood that flowed from his hands and feet.

I didn't know God that well, but I understood that He must have loved us very much to give up His son to die for our sins. Why did we need God to die for our sins before we could enter heaven? Although I understood the concept that there were consequences to our choices and a penalty for our sins, I did not realize how serious God was about sin and that the penalty for any sin was death. I could see death as a penalty for the really big sins. But how could death be the penalty for a white lie or the mistakes I made unintentionally? My mind did not fathom the perfect holiness of God and that He regarded any sin as so offensive to His perfection that He pronounced the judicial verdict to be death. Against this incredible high standard of holiness that I could never attain was a just God who could not let sin go unpunished but a loving God who chose to take the penalty of death in my place. I heard this message. I read it several times in the literature of my bible classes at the mission school. However, the full impact of what God did for me did not sink in till years later.

The story of God's son leaving heaven's throne to come to earth to die for my sins so I could receive the gift of living forever in the presence of God's perfect holiness is a story that changes your life, if you truly understand it. I must not have fully understood the greatest story that ever took place on planet earth because it never once occurred to me to say, "God, you ransomed my life. My life does not belong to me anymore, it belongs to you. What do you want to do with my life?"

I did not know then that the Acts of the Apostles was a book in the Bible that intentionally ended without a closing chapter. The book ends with the words, "For two whole years Paul stayed in his own rented house and welcomed all who came to see him. Boldly and without hindrance he preached the kingdom of God and taught about the Lord Jesus." The reader was left hanging as to what happened to Paul after two years. How did the story end? I did not know that this open ended last chapter was God's way to tell us that He is still writing the end of His story through the acts of those who believe in Him. I did not know God has dreams of His own which He entrusts to His followers.

THE LONELINESS WE FEEL IS WHEN NO ONE WILL WALK WITH US

THE SCHOOL BELL RANG. I PUT BACK THE HYMNAL and ran to stand in line with my class. All the classes lined up on the playground. In front of us were concrete bleachers at the top of which stood the principal. Her name was Sister Rosangeles. She was a blue-eyed Italian nun who was a little over 5-foot tall. The entire school was run by the nuns and women teachers. They looked so petite but they ran every program perfectly. Once in a while, there might be a man teacher but he was considered an oddity.

Sister Rosangeles taught me about loving people. On looking back, I realize I must have taken up a lot of her time. All the questions my parents did not have time to answer, I asked Sister Rosangeles. As I wrestled with the problems I saw in the world, she became my walking encyclopedia for world solutions. She would say to me, "Dear child, does that mind ever stop?" Then she would say, "Just be like Jesus and love people!" Her words seemed too simple then. I did not realize she was echoing God's words from the Bible when He said in 1 Corinthians 13:8-13, "Love never fails. But where there are prophecies, they will cease; where there are tongues, they will be stilled; where there is knowledge, it will pass away. For we know in part and we prophesy in part, but when perfection comes, the imperfect disappears. When I was a child, I talked like a child, I thought like a child, I reasoned like a child. When I became a man, I put child-ish ways behind me. Now we see but a poor reflection as in a mirror; then we shall see face to face. Now I know in part; then I shall know fully, even as I am fully known. And now these three remain: faith, hope and love. But the greatest of these is love."

I don't remember much of what I asked Sister Rosangeles or what she answered. Perhaps the questions weren't that important. Perhaps even the answers weren't that important. Perhaps what was important was my knowing that if I had a question, there was someone I could go to. What was important was my knowing that Sister Rosangeles would always be there to offer me an answer.

Sometimes I wonder if the weekly e-devotional Inspire Women sends out every Monday morning to those on our mailing list, grew from this seed in the past. Would Inspire Women confront the questions we struggle with in life and offer answers from God's Word? How do we rise above betrayal? How do we make sense of our pain? How do we trust God when our lives are unraveling? When the confusion of life overwhelms us, the beacon of hope is in knowing there might be an answer somewhere. The light in the darkness is a voice that reminds us that someone relates to our pain, someone validates our feelings, someone is not afraid to ask God for His answers to our questions. The loneliness we feel is when no one will walk with us in the midst of our confusion. Within the human spirit is a need to belong, a need to connect, a need to know that our questions matter, a hope that our questions will one day find resolution.

In the city of Hong Kong, the dominant Christian denomination was Catholic so that was the denomination I was exposed to. Do I remember any of the doctrine? I don't think I understood much of what was being taught. What I recall are not the factual details I memorized about religion in my childhood days. All I remember is how those who proclaimed Christ made me feel. When I came to the United States and God took me through different Protestant denominations, I felt like a homing pigeon that could immediately sense those with the love of Christ.

I have found that the spirit of Christ exists in every Christian denomination. The united body of Jesus Christ is one that He formed from His shed blood, broken body, and sacrifice. There is a unity that exists among those who have understood His sacrifice and who desire to live for Him.

Although there are debates among denominations that are valid and help us to build the foundation of our faith, I wonder if some arguments find fertile soil when nothing pressing is going on. When the U.S. army was fighting in Iraq, I don't believe any soldier in the heat of battle asked, "Are you from the North or are you from the South?" In the heat of battle, no one cares about things that do not have life and death consequences. Instead, when your life is on the line, you celebrate that there is a soldier next to you who is wearing the same uniform and represents the United Sates of America. You just pray they fight well. You mourn when they are shot down. You grieve when they die because no matter what your personal differences, you know you are one man down and you have lost a friend.

I FELT SO HELPLESS TO RESCUE HER DIGNITY

I WAS IN THE SAME SCHOOL FROM ELEMENTARY school through high school. My class room experience exposed me to yet another culture. Because Hong Kong was still a British colony at the time I was in school, all the instruction was in English. I could take Chinese as a foreign language. I picked French instead. So here I was, a Chinese kid immersed in a British education system learning to speak British and French. How very strange! But on looking back, I see that all things work together for good for those who trust God. I learned that language helps you understand a culture. For example, if you went shopping in France and a saleslady showed you an item in red and you didn't like red, you would never say in French, "I don't like red." Instead, you might say, "Thank you so much but I prefer blue." Learning different languages helps you to step into someone else's world and ways of doing things. What was unique in your upbringing? Is there something God was growing in you to shape you for your moment in His story?

When I think of my elementary school years, two incidents are etched in my memory. Both took place when I was in second grade. One of the girls in my class had an upset stomach. The reason we knew this was because the teacher said out-loud, "What is that smell? Did someone go to the bathroom in here?" Everyone looked around and then someone pointed to the girl sitting next to her. The girl's name was Teresa. She was a tiny little girl. All I knew was, I always felt like a giant next to her. The teacher asked one of the girls to go and get one of the women who took care of the school facilities and bathrooms. That woman showed up in our class making it known to everyone, how inconvenienced she was by someone who went in their pants while sitting in the classroom. "For heaven's sake," she said, "Why didn't you have the sense to go to the bathroom?" She had in her hands a bucket and a handful of toilet paper. She grabbed Teresa and in front of the class, she told her to take off her pants. Then, she pushed her to bend over and wiped her bottom with the toilet paper. Teresa tried to cover herself but the woman became irritated and told her to stay bent over while she wiped. The girls in the class started to giggle. The teacher told the class to be quiet and to concentrate on their work. I saw how Teresa's face grew redder and redder. She was one of the shyest girls in the class. She hardly spoke a word to anyone. And here she was with her privacy exposed for the world to ridicule. I shut my eyes and I could almost feel myself stop breathing. I just wanted the clock to stop so this moment in time would be erased and forgotten. I felt so helpless to rescue her dignity. How could this be happening? I learned that even in the midst of an environment that proclaimed the love of Christ, fallen humanity continually destroys what God intended. What do we do with the events in our lives that broke our spirit during our formative vulnerable years? I didn't have an answer for Teresa then, but I have an answer now.

Against all the horrid stories on planet earth is the story of God sending His one and only son to die for our sins. God allowed His son to be stripped naked. He allowed him to be hung on a cross for the crowds to see. He who had no sin bore the penalty of our sins. In whatever shame or injustice I experienced in my life, I know God has felt my pain. Moreover, He bore the shame on the cross in my place. As badly as I felt for Teresa, would I have offered to take her place?

As you were reading about what happened to Teresa, would you have offered to take her place? Yet, while we were still sinners and were far from God, He came from heaven to earth to take our shame and to allow Himself to be nailed naked on a cross. Our experiences, as hard as they may be, give us a glimpse into the pain God endured when He chose to die for us. He did not go to the cross while I was serving and loving Him. He went to the cross when I had no clue who He was and while there was no guarantee that I would ever love him back.

Once I begin to understand the sacrifice God was willing to bear on my behalf, my story pales by comparison. My suffering, then, finds meaning when I am willing to lose my story in the greater story God is telling about His Son. Giving God's story center stage helps me to put my suffering in perspective. The human tendency is to make ourselves center stage. The question we must settle for ourselves is this: "Which story will consume and drive me in my life? My story or God's story?" Can I use my personal loss and suffering as a way to direct attention to the greater suffering Christ bore on my behalf?

Another incident I witnessed was during recess. One of the girls was crying and told the teacher that someone broke her shoes. I could see that all the stitches on her shoe were coming apart. In fact, the shoe was barely on her foot because the entire seam on one side of the shoe was open. She said, "Someone stepped on my foot and tore up my shoe." The teacher said, "No one broke your shoe! Don't blame others. Tell your parents to buy you new shoes." The bell for the end of recess rang. I saw the girl dragging her foot across the ground to keep the shoe from falling off. The next day, I didn't see her in school anymore. I don't know what became of her. I wonder if she was too embarrassed to admit that her parents did not have the money to buy her new shoes?

GOD'S LOVE WILL WIN IN THE END

I DON'T KNOW WHY SOME TEACHERS WERE UNKIND BUT I know God allowed them in my life. Perhaps, it was to show me that in spite of the unkindness, God's love will win in the end.

Christians and Christianity was not always what I had hoped it to be. When I look back at my life, there were times when it felt like the church was my enemy. God allowed me to go through a lot of challenges I did not think I could handle. I remember I was so terribly lonely in this country, I decided to go home. I had a passport but it never dawned on me that I needed a visa to re-enter Hong Kong. So, here I was at the airport in Los Angeles and the flight attendant would not let me get on the plane. She said I had to get a visa.

I tried to get to the British consulate in Los Angeles.

Here I was at the age of 19. Imagine me walking down the streets of Los Angeles with my guitar. Yes, I lugged around this guitar. I think I looked like a flower child. I felt so totally lost and pitiful. I remember seeing a church and the very sight of it gave me comfort. So I climbed up the flight of stairs that led to the front door. I pushed on the door thinking I might get some replenishment by sitting in God's presence. Well, this was Los Angeles and I didn't realize that they locked the church doors because of vandalism. So, I couldn't get into the church. I found myself sitting outside on the stone steps with my guitar and thinking, "Wow! I can't even get to God!"

I remember there was a season when I was seriously searching for God's purpose for my life. It was during that time that my path crossed with that of a young Christian leader. I so admired him because he knew the Bible like the back of his hand. Whenever we had a discussion about life, he could argue from Scripture and quoted verses at me. It was also this Christian leader, whom I trusted, who led me to a remote place where he sexually molested me. How could he have appeared so holy on the outside? I felt like such a fool because I had trusted this person completely. I was too embarrassed to say anything so I went about life as if nothing had ever happened. Meanwhile, I wondered if there were any genuine Christians. Does anyone truly love people the way Jesus did? Or was religion simply an act to look holy on the outside while hiding a perversion on the inside?

During the early years of my Christian journey, I had

no knowledge of God through His Word. Although I had memorized large portions of the Bible, I never knew how to release the power of God's Word for my life. I thought there was power in just memorizing the words. I didn't realize the power was released only when I step out in faith to put God's words into action. I knew God was love but I thought He lived in a church building. When I couldn't get into the church in Los Angeles, it felt like even God was distant and the doors were shut. I can imagine now how God was looking down from heaven. I can imagine how His Holy Spirit was right there with me, but I had not learned to recognize His presence.

I have often wondered why God did not send some lightning flash from heaven to say, "Don't despair! Here I am!" I have since concluded that God has a plan. He allows us to go through the desert so we can be a testimony to others that there is an oasis around the corner. In our minds, we feel like we are dying in our drought. From God's perspective, He is not worried because He can see down the line. He already saw my future. He saw Inspire Women. He allowed these heartbreaking experiences because it would grow compassion in my heart for my sisters who feel displaced in life and need an anchor for their lives. I have since learned that what God allows into our lives is part of the story He desires to tell through us. There is a master plan. God has a plan for your life as well and you will see the fullness of His intentions in His perfect timing. Do you believe this?

MAKING A FOOL OF MYSELF

P ERHAPS, BECAUSE MY MOTHER NEVER BECAME A star, she pushed me to do what she always wanted. Why did she want to be a star? When money is tight, stardom is simply a means to an end. I remember, every year, one of the biggest events in the city was the Hong Kong Talent Quest. Thousands would enter, hoping to be the newly discovered star of the year. From those who entered, I could tell that many did not have the talent but they were willing to try anything to get a break in life. They looked to stardom as a way to support the family. They tried to showcase any uniqueness in themselves as a way to stand out and to survive. I don't know why I joined the Hong Kong Talent Quest. I think perhaps I was trying to give my mother her dream. I did not know then that God created me for His dreams, not hers.

I recruited my sister and a friend. My mother made us outfits and we called ourselves "The Single Girls". We performed the song titled "The Single Girls". Amazingly, we made it past seventeen hundred entries till we reached the grand finals. We had a dance routine that went with our song. We came in second. If we had come in first, we would have received a recording contract. The next year, I joined again but this time I was on my own. I entered under the stage name, "Terri Anne". Did I think I could hide under a different name? I found my face on the front page of the newspaper. From all the contestants, why did the photographer choose to feature my act?

When I look back at this experience, I ask myself, "What in the world were you thinking?" I didn't have the talent to sustain a music career. I wasn't even interested in a music career. But even through this ridiculous incident, I learned that God conforms all things for the purpose of His will. Years later, when I was asked if I would teach God's Word on television, without hesitation, I answered, "Yes." The marching orders were, "Ten shows, one for each day of the week for two weeks." I was to arrive at that station and to bring a change of clothes because the series would be taped back to back. The change of clothes would give the appearance that I was teaching on a different day. Had I ever done a program on television? No. Did I have any idea how to do a program on television? No. But dare I give God less than I was willing to do in my yesteryears when I would dive head first into projects I knew nothing about? With God on my side, there would be no limit to what He could do.

At the studio, I watched the taping that was ahead of me. I noticed there were cue cards that tell you how much time you have left. I noticed you must end your sentence on the count of one. You had to think quickly and you had to think backwards as you constructed your concluding sentences so as to end with an inspirational note at the count of "Five, four, three, two, one, cut!" I thought perhaps I could by chance accomplish this for one show but to expect to do this for ten shows in a row was a stretch.

I also learned that the personnel at the studio get upset if you have to re-tape your segment. They expected the guests on their shows to get things right on "Take one". But God knew these details.

In Isaiah 30:21, God said, "Whether you turn to the right or to the left, your ears will hear a voice behind you, saying, "This is the way; walk in it." I taped ten shows over a two day period. Each finished perfectly on the count of one. I was relieved. The crew said to me, "You must have done this before." I just smiled and left the studio. Inside I was thinking, "I am spent! I hope I never have to do that again!" People can talk about faith all they want. I have found that as long as you are in human flesh, your stomach still cramps when you know you are expected to deliver the goods and you have no idea how you are going to do it. In the midst of the greatest faith, there is still that tiny question, "Will God come through for me?"

I was asked to do another five shows. I didn't know then that God was custom tailoring my training program. He was teaching me to step into uncharted territory. He was teaching me that when there is no one there to lead you by the hand, He will walk with you. To those He calls, He will empower. In Christ alone, we have all that we need to finish the work He entrusts to us. The question is, "Do you believe it? And will you receive it?" If so, then you are God's miracle waiting to happen. What is God doing in your life? Is it time for a new beginning? Is it time to take a chance so you can leave the prison of your past to step into God's new beginning for your life? Oh, may the new story begin!

3

New Beginnings Begin With You

When my mother burst into tears, I wasn't sure why she was so upset. She came home and found me in the middle of a sewing project. I had gotten it into my head to make a stuffed bed for my dog. The project consisted of sewing a large sack and stuffing it with whatever filling I could find that would create a plump feel. I had found an old pillow in a storage room and cut it up to empty its contents into my sack. To my surprise, there were feathers everywhere. I had no idea the pillow was made of goose down. My mother walked in on the scene while I was trying to capture all the white lightweight down that was floating in the air like snow. At first, I thought my mother was upset because of the mess I had made but I soon found out I had opened a wound in her heart.

MY MOTHER'S LIFE WAS FILLED WITH SECRETS

I FOUND OUT THE PILLOW BELONGED TO MY BROTHER. This was a brother that I did not meet until he was eighteen and I was two. My mother's life was filled with secrets, some of which she revealed to me, some of which she carried with her to her grave. I found out the pillow was the only baby item my mother saved from her days with my brother.

I also found out my mother's father had a history of unemployment. I never met him because I never met any of my mother's relatives. The gates to China were shut to the rest of the world while I was growing up. So, I knew I had family, but I had no idea who they were. I did not grow up with my father's relatives either because, though my father was Chinese, he was born in Indonesia. I don't know what it feels like to have a grandmother or a grandfather. When other children in school spoke of spending time with their grandparents, I had no idea what it felt like to have a doting grandparent. When my friends complained about having to juggle schedules in order to meet for a family gathering, I wished I had some of their inconveniences.

My mother was the oldest in her family and during the months when there was no income, she took it upon herself to go to the home of her relatives begging for food.

She once said to me, "You will know who your friends are when you need a bowl of rice." Some of her relatives would ridicule her and say, "So is your father out of work again? Why can't that man hold down a job?" They would then hand her some rice while making her feel ashamed on the inside.

IN THAT ROOM, HE RAPED HER

M<small>Y MOTHER WAS FIFTEEN WHEN SHE WENT TO</small> work in a hotel in order to bring in some income for the family. Though she had other siblings, they never offered to help. Instead, they put more financial burden on her father. She was the only one who shared his burden.

While she was cleaning one of the rooms, a business-man who had paid for the room came in before she was through. My mother was a petite teenager with a beautiful face. She had long black hair that she wore pulled back in a bun. Her features were delicate, her eyes were round and dark, her smile lit up her face. She had one of those personalities where she would walk into a room and everyone would notice. People always gravitated towards my mother because she was full of creative ideas. On top of that she had a mischievous spirit in her that always dared fate. People were intrigued with her because she believed in the impossible. I don't know what she said to this man but I can just imagine that when he saw her, he saw a pretty little Chinese girl who was in a secluded room. My mother said when he locked the door, she knew she was in trouble. She tried to push past him but, he overpowered her. Though my mother screamed for help, no one heard her. In that room, he raped her.

When my mother told me her story, I could picture her walking home with this big dark secret that she could not tell anyone. She straightened up her hair and pretended like nothing had happened. She knew that in China, her future for marriage was over. She was no longer a virgin, and she was a disgrace to her family. She would never dare tell anyone in her family for fear that they would throw her out of the house. So she said nothing.

A year later, she stumbled upon a Caucasian business man in town who was looking for someone to teach him Chinese. He owned a restaurant in China. My mother applied for the job because her family was desperate for income. At that time, she was sixteen and this man was twenty years older than she was. In a short time, he became totally smitten with her. He asked her to marry him. My mother felt she had no other future because of what had happened to her in that hotel room. Besides, this man was patient and kind and treated her like his little China doll. He absolutely adored her and wanted to take care of her and all her family. So she married him. She described her life as settled and happy. Her advice for my life was always to marry a man who adores you and makes you feel like a princess.

Soon after she got married, my mother became pregnant, and she had my brother when she was still sixteen.

This was also during the time of World War II. The Japanese had invaded China, and my mother's new husband was put in prison. I'm not sure why. I believe my mother said it was because he was a foreigner and the army was suspicious of him. She went to visit him in prison with her baby for many months. Then one day, when my brother was two, she went to the prison and the soldiers told her not to return anymore because her husband was no longer alive. She never saw the body. There was never a funeral. I can imagine her leaving the prison with her two year old, knowing that a chapter of her life had ended.

"GOD IS NOT BLIND. THOSE WHO CHOOSE FOR HIM WILL PROSPER!"

MY MOTHER'S LIFE WAS FILLED WITH NEW BEGIN-NINGS and sudden endings. She had a son who was not accepted in her society because he had foreign blood in him. My brother used to dye his hair with shoe polish to hide his blonde highlights. My mother was a widow with a child who was an outcast in her society. Fortunately, her deceased husband left her money to live on or else she would have been totally at the mercy of those around her. The money he left her served as her protection. At least, she was able to support herself and her son.

The next big event in her life was after the war when the communist movement in China was growing. In 1947, when the communists started sweeping through China, my mother pleaded with her family to leave. They were afraid to leave because they wanted to hold on to what was familiar. So, she said, "One of us must leave. At least one of us will be on the outside and can send help in." When she left for Hong Kong, my brother was eight years old. Her intentions were to get my brother as soon as she found a job and a place to stay. But the communists swept through the country faster than she anticipated and the gates were shut. She did not see her son again until he was eighteen.

I can just imagine my mother getting on the train and waving goodbye to her son. Even today, my brother remembers the day he watched the train take off with his mother on it. To this day, when he watches farewell scenes in movies, the images trigger something deep inside him and he'll find himself sobbing like a baby. I can't imagine what it was like for my mother to be away from her child. I only remember her to be a practical woman who was forced to bury her feelings. She would do what was best for the family no matter what personal sacrifice it required of her. She sent money home to my brother while she tried to make it on her own in a new city with no friends or connections. It was during this time that she met my father. Soon after, she married and had my sister and me.

Oh, what sorrow I must have released in her when I cut up my brother's baby pillow! It was her only keepsake from the time she had with him. How much she must have grieved over all the years she never had with him. How much she must have wanted to know if he was doing all right but felt so totally helpless to return to him. He was raised by the Chinese red guards. He said he recited the thoughts of Chairman Mao the same way Christians memorized Scripture. Today, he is a born again Christian and is the Senior Vice President of Fidelity Investments in Boston, Massachusetts. In spite of the fact that he had no family network, he grew up to exhibit the same kindness as his father and the same self sacrificial love of his mother. He does not waste time holding grudges or being resentful of relatives who were unkind to him during his childhood years. His life reminds me of my mother who often said, "God is not blind. Those who choose for Him will prosper."

NEVER BUILD ON LAND THAT IS TEMPORARY!

WHILE MY MOTHER WAS IN HONG KONG, SHE received letters from the family in China, telling her that the family home had been divided because there was no such thing as private property. Four different families lived in the house. People were afraid to say what they really felt, not knowing what the political affiliation of anyone else in that house was. One day, my uncle said something unflattering about the government, and then one of the people in the house must have reported him.

The Red Guards appeared at the door and escorted him away. The family did not know of his whereabouts for two and a half years. When he returned, he was a different man. My mother said he had been re-educated.

In 1887 Hong Kong had been given to England by China as part of a war treaty settlement for 100 years. My mother knew that Hong Kong was to be returned by England to China in June of 1997. It was with fear that my mother anticipated the coming of this date. I grew up always being reminded that I was living in a country that was temporary. How does one live in a country that is temporary? How does one live in a country with a built-in expiration date? Have you ever needed life to be built on a foundation that no human or event could take from you?

In anticipation of the imminent Communist Chinese takeover, my mother wanted to carve a path of escape for her family. But, she had one major problem. She had no grounds for immigration. She could not say to another country, "Let me in because of my skills or education." She never went past a third grade education. She could not say, "Let me in because of my finances." She read in the paper that if you had $250,000 in the bank, you increase your chances to get a visa to live in a different country. She did not have that kind of money. She could not say to a country, "Let me in because of my family sponsorship" because she knew no one in the free land. But she believed with all her heart that God is good and in the end, the righteous will win. So, against all odds, she an uneducated woman offered God what she had and began to train her children in their academics, hoping that it would be through our excellence that we would find a way to the Promise Land of America.

In 1960, in a desperate attempt to get my brother out of China, my mother appealed to the sympathies of the Communist Government and he was granted a temporary visa. As soon as he arrived, she told him he was never going back. He said, "In that case, I want to go as far away from China as I can. I want to go to America." She told him that if he studied, she would try to find a way to raise the money.

Two years later, my brother won a scholarship to an American University. My mother sold all that she had to buy him a one way ticket. So, here she was, at the airport, saying goodbye to the son that she had just reunited with. My brother began to cry and my mother said, "Don't cry because this is not a sad time. This is a happy time. This is the beginning of a dream come true." I believe that deep in her heart, she knew that this might be the last time she would see his face but she was willing to release him to live the dream she always wanted for herself and for her children. Although I did not know my brother very well, I knew my mother placed many of her hopes in him. She always told me he was a gifted child with a big heart. His name was Bobby. My mother said it was the English translation for the Chinese word "Treasure".

After my brother left, I remember that she prayed for him and she begged God to take care of her son. She knew that in six month's time his money would run out, and she had nothing left to send him. Meanwhile, she continued to drill my sister and me in our academics.

Years later, my brother took me to the neighborhood where he lived while attending college. He did not have money for rent for an apartment. So, he paid for sleeping space and rented a cot in a run down apartment in New York city. He worked two jobs while going through school. He told me when he interviewed for his first job in Chinatown, the restaurant owner asked him if he had experience wrapping wontons. He said he did. The owner found out very quickly that while the other workers could wrap wontons at lightning speed, it took my brother three minutes to do one. So, he was instantly fired. He immediately went down the road to the next restaurant. When the next owner asked him if he had experience, he said, "Absolutely and named the restaurant he had just come from!" He quickly became one of the top waiters and the tips he earned paid his bills through school. He never asked my mother for one more penny. Instead, he carried with him a piece of jewelry my mother had given him. She had told him, "If you run out of money, sell this." Years later, he still had that piece of jewelry. I don't know if he was ever down to his last penny, but he never sold what my mother gave him.

My mother drummed into me the fact that you should never want to build your life on a temporary foundation. No matter how glamorous life may appear, my mother always looked towards where life was heading. The moral of the story was, "Never build on land that will not be here one day." Even as a child, the concept of building on a permanent foundation made sense to me. So, while my friends were chasing dreams in the city, all my attention was focused on reaching the free land of America.

For the longest time, I always thought of permanence in terms of a physical land or space. I strove to acquire what was tangible and visible that I could hold in my hands. I did not realize then that my true security and freedom will come when I am no longer dependent on anything physical that could possibly be destroyed on this earth. I discovered later that I will find my permanent foundation when I build my life on God's Word. He then becomes my foundation and my roots. With God's Word as my roots, I am transplanted into a family tree that is eternal and represents a legacy with an eternal agenda. With God's Word as my roots, He becomes my foundation, and in Him, I will find rock beneath my feet and a place from which to soar. No longer am I dependent on the physical items or relationships on earth. I am truly free to go with God wherever He desires to send me. Jesus said in Matthew 7:24-27, "Therefore everyone who hears these words of mine and puts them into practice is like a wise man who built his house on the rock. The rain came down, the streams rose, and the winds blew and beat against that house; yet it did not fall, because it had its foundation on the rock. But everyone who hears these words of mine and does not put them into practice is like a foolish man who built his house on sand. The rain came down, the streams rose, and the winds blew and beat against that house, and it fell with a great crash." Years later, I discovered how much God owned on this earth. My security then, is not in what I own but in what He owns. When I live according to His Word and for His purpose, He miraculously frees up His resources to enable me to finish the work He entrusted to me.

YOU CANNOT LIVE SOMEONE ELSE'S DREAM

MY SISTER'S NAME IS ROSITA. PEOPLE USE TO KID my Dad because he had two girls with Spanish names. It was unusual for two Chinese girls to be named Rosita and Anita.

Following my brother's footsteps, both my sister and I won full scholarships to American universities. We were both scheduled to leave in the summer of 1974. My sister was two years older than me and could have left earlier. However, she chose to wait until I graduated so we could leave the country together. She filled her time with taking secretarial courses. I remember growing up, my sister would get mad at me every time I borrowed her clothes. She accused me of stretching them or losing them. She told me once I was not allowed to take anything of hers for the rest of my life. I always knew my sister just talked tough, but her heart was tender towards me. She always tried to protect me. I know that her waiting for me to graduate so she could leave the country at the same time was one of the ways she was trying to protect her baby sister.

In February of 1974, five months before we were scheduled to leave, I heard a shrill cry that woke me from my sleep. It was early in the morning when the day was still thick with darkness. I woke my sister up and followed timidly behind her as we groped our way through the darkness. I stayed in the living room while she went on into the kitchen and I heard my father's voice say in a panting way, "Quick! Get a knife! Cut her down!" as he was holding up the body of my mother to keep her weight from choking her further, for she had hung herself from the rafters.

I stood in that living room and watched my father and my sister carry her body in. As I stared at her lifeless form, my body grew numb and my blood grew cold with disbelief because "How could it be? How could it be that the woman who dared to dream the impossible dream of America could somehow lose that dream for herself?"

For weeks I walked around in shock. I went to school and sat through my classes hiding from the crowd that the ground beneath my feet had collapsed. Days after my mother's death we found a box containing several pieces of jewelry. She would save up her money and buy gold and diamonds believing they would hold their value over time. In the box was a note that read, "This is for my son and my daughters for their future in America."

When did she leave the note? How long had she

planned her exit? How could she have planned such an exit without my being remotely aware of her decision? The dream of reaching America was one she had planted in me and one we were going to execute together. The idea was, as long as we were together, we would make it. Our small nuclear family was the only family we had. I felt like a big part of my roots was gone.

What caused her to lose hope? Did she believe her children would not return to get her? Now that we were leaving, did she feel her mission was over? What exactly was going through her head? Questions, questions, and more questions.

I found a book she was reading titled, "The Imitation of Christ." It felt very eerie looking through the pages of a book which was the last book she held in her hands. In the book she had highlighted the words in John 15:13 which read, "Greater love has no one than this, that he lay down his life for his friends." Did she think her death would purchase our favor with God? Oh, how dangerous it is when we misinterpret God's Word. God offered His son as a final sacrifice. There was nothing else my mother could have added to the sacrifice. What God wants from us is faith. Was my mother trying to bargain with God? Or perhaps, her past simply caught up with her. Did the ashes from buried dreams that never materialized suffocate the life in her? When U.S. Immigration denied her exit papers to leave the country with her children, was the thought of being separated from her daughters too much to bear? Was her suicide an act of despair? Was it an act of insanity? Why did she lose hope in the God she trusted for so many years? On and on my mind asked questions I had no answers to.

I learned that suicide is a permanent solution to a temporary problem. With the takeover of the Communists in 1997, things were not the way she had expected. People have even gone back to Hong Kong to take advantage of economic opportunities. Shortly after her death, my brother had re-petitioned and my father was granted an exit visa a year and a half later. He now lives in America. That dream would have been hers. I learned that even when all the odds are against you, you must trust God to write the end of the story.

I had not heard my brother's voice since the day he left for the United States. Although making a phone call today seems common, it was a big event in our family to make an international call. When we called our brother to tell him the news, I appealed to him to return to Hong Kong. My brother had been gone for thirteen years. During that time, his whole focus had been to save his funds so he could help the family reach America. He was extremely frugal with his finances and sacrificially put aside the money to pay the immigration attorneys and just in case we needed extra funds to resettle in America. When he returned for my mother's funeral, I could tell that his heart was breaking. All these years he was waiting for the big day when we would arrive together as a family. He had hired attorneys to work on our immigration papers. Was standing by the coffin of my mother the way the story was ending?

I always knew my brother to be practical, the same way my mother was. It was as if he had been forced all his life to make the right decisions no matter what he was feeling on the inside. He immediately took over the guidance of my sister and me. His goal was to bring us to the free land of America and to help us build a new future. My brother was a man of few words. He simply always did the right things to protect his family. In spite of his few words, the one thing I have always heard him say was, "Mother had a hard life."

When I boarded the plane for America, I was seventeen. I remember waving goodbye to my father as he stood there all alone, knowing that he would return to an empty home. As I sat on the plane, I remember putting my arms around myself, imagining them to be the arms of God, begging God to give me the courage to enter my future.

When I set foot on the free land of America, I was filled with euphoria at having reached the dream that began in my mother's heart. At the same time, I was filled with a grief that no words could describe. I was like an athlete who had trained for years in the Olympics and here I was holding my gold medal, and my coach was not with me. I was like a soldier who had been in a long battle and here I was crossing the line to victory and my general was shot down at the border. And I found myself going through my memory bank to piece together the time I had shared with my mother, so I could put together some kind of a script for the rest of my life.

What do you do when the person you dreamed the dream with is no longer with you? New beginnings begin with you. You cannot live someone else's dream. You cannot read off someone else's script. If you do, after a while, you will be living on fumes. Although other people may be part of your journey, at some point, your journey must become your own or else you won't know how the story is supposed to end.

MOM, WHERE ARE YOU?

THAT FIRST SUMMER IN AMERICA, I STAYED WITH MY brother. His wife, Kathy, introduced me to life in the United States. When she first made me a peanut butter and jelly sandwich, I actually had my heart set on a bowl of noodles. When she made me a tuna sandwich, I had to adjust to fish from a can as compared to picking out the fish from the fish tank in the water and watching it de-scaled and cleaned right in front of me. I don't remember much from my time in my brother's home except that it was very quiet and peaceful compared to the pace in Hong Kong. I was used to hearing the cars go by outside my window in Hong Kong but at my brother's house, I did not hear the honking of cars or people yelling at each other. I could not hear hawkers from the marketplace. Kathy kept an immaculate home. Everything around me had its place while the world inside me was unraveling.

After a month, my sister and I began making final plans to travel to college. I had won a scholarship from a college in California. My sister's scholarship was to a college in Mississippi. My brother was concerned that his sisters were raised in an all girls' mission school with little knowledge of how things worked in the real world. He used to kid us by saying that we thought we got pregnant by sitting on a toilet seat. He was worried about my going to California, so he called my sister's college to see if I could get in. My sister and I ended up going to an all women's college in Columbus, Mississippi.

It was more economical to travel by bus, so my sister and I took a Greyhound from New York City to Columbus, Mississippi. I had my two suitcases with me that contained all my belongings. I remember we had to change bus in Atlanta, Georgia. It was two in the morning. I was whining about being tired and was complaining about carrying my suitcases. My sister told me to shut up and she carried my suitcases for me.

As we were waiting for the bus to leave, I was standing by myself in the terminal. A young man in his twenties came up to me and said, "There is a man across the street and he said you have some money for me." I had no idea what he was talking about. So I just looked at him and pretended I could not speak English. He then said to me, "You don't speak English, do you?" I shrugged my shoulders as if I didn't understand. So, he walked away. When my sister returned from the ladies room, I told her what had happened. She scolded me for being so naïve and almost getting myself in trouble. She said the man was probably dealing in drugs. I got scared and did not let her leave my side after that incident. She was always the tougher one, the smarter one. I always saw myself as being safe under her wings.

After we arrived on campus, we registered for our classes. When I kept receiving letters from my father telling me how lonely he was, I wanted to rush home as soon as I could. At the same time, I was plagued by my promise to my mother to secure my education. So, I tested out of several classes and received credit for the years of French I took in Hong Kong. I also appealed to the Dean to take twenty four credit hours a semester. He told me no one at the college had ever taken that many hours. I told him about my father and how I was trying to get through as soon as I could. He told me I would risk losing my scholarship if my G.P.A. fell. We made a deal that if I could maintain my G.P.A. he would approve my overload. I plunged into my academics and finished a four-year program in two years. I was in such a hurry to finish but I had no idea where I was going. Then God planted a seed and began to respond to the prayers of a mother to protect her children, though she was not here to see it. In the midst of my frantic pace, God orchestrated events to walk me into His plan. On looking back at my life, I stand amazed how God was never in a hurry. He knew exactly where He was heading.

In my first year in college, I met a freshman. Her name was Christine Petcher. She just happened to be a missionary's daughter. Her parents had just returned from planting churches in Africa. Her father was the town's physician and a deacon in the local church. Christine invited me home every weekend and every American holiday. I even spent a whole summer with her. While I was with her, I saw people totally surrendered to God in all their time, their resources, and their energies. I wanted so much to be like them but I couldn't. Deep in my heart, I was haunted by the memory of my mother. I didn't even know what the script was, but I wanted to live my mother's script for my life. So I said, "I cannot surrender my life to God." The whole idea of "surrender" felt too vague for me. I wanted to control the details of my life. I did not trust God enough to allow Him to write the end of my story.

In my second year, I transferred to the University of Mississippi. God planted another seed. I was wandering around campus one weekend and I saw a bus being loaded up with students. Out of curiosity, I went up and asked, "Who are you and where are you going?" They said, "We're Campus Crusade for Christ. We're going on a retreat. Why don't you come with us?" I said, "I don't have anything with me. I have no blanket, no toothbrush, no money." They said, "We'll provide everything. Just come with us." I don't know why, but I got onto that bus and then I was stuck because I had no way to get back. But that weekend, I was reminded about the God who gave up His one and only son for me. From those days in the chapel in my mission school in Hong Kong, I had accepted the gift of Jesus for the salvation of my soul but I had yet to learn to walk in His power for my life. Could I possibly trust a God who has proven His love through the sacrifice of His Son to heal my heart and to give me a new dream for my life? Could He possibly understand my pain considering that He experienced letting go of His son? The whole idea of letting go of a loved one opened up my wounds. I wept for my mother and I wept for my father and I wept for myself. And God was able to console me, but only temporarily for without knowing how to get into the Bible on my own, I did not know how to glean the instruction from His Word to sustain me. I had no concept for what He was doing on earth and I did not realize I could trust Him with the rest of my life.

When I transferred to the University of Mississippi, my sister would come to visit me over the weekend. It was a four hour bus ride between our two campuses. I remember one weekend, she called me up and she was in tears. She was rushing to get to the bus but was stung by a wasp. So she had rushed to the infirmary and as a result, she missed the bus. The next weekend, she came up, I could not spend that much time with her because I was studying for a test. She stayed with some of my friends who lived in an apartment off campus. I was living in the dorms on campus.

It was about one in the morning when I received a phone call from my friends from the apartment complex. They said my sister was sitting in the middle of the road. They could not get her to return to the apartment. She was drunk and she was crying her heart out. When I came out to the apartment, I heard her wailing, "Mom, where are you? Mom, I tried to be strong for Anita and for Daddy but Mom, I can't do it. Mom, please help me!" I stood in the shadows and watched as my friends finally coaxed her back to the apartment. She never knew I was there. I knew she always wanted to appear strong for me. I didn't want her to know that I had seen her in a moment of weakness. The whole while she was saying to my friends, "Please don't tell Anita. She's trying to study for a test." After I saw that she was back in the apartment, I went back to the campus.

Till today, that scene is etched vividly in my mind. I saw that as much as my mother loved us, she had not given us what we needed to walk into the rest of our lives. I saw the desperation in my sister when she did not know how to go on with life. I wonder today if this experience is why the heart of Inspire Women is to put the rock of God's Word beneath our sisters' feet. We believe that if there is one gift we can give our sisters that will carry them through their lives, it would be the gift of knowing how to get into God's Word on their own and to find His purpose for their lives. Although we cannot control or know what will happen in the future, we believe that if they can just get to God's Word to hear His marching orders, then we have connected ourselves to an eternal lifeline and no human or event can ever shake our world.

I JUST WANTED THE PAIN TO STOP

IN 1976, I GRADUATED FROM A FOUR YEAR PROGRAM in two years. I was finishing my last class at the age of 19. Shortly before I graduated, I received a letter from my father asking for my permission to remarry. Deep in my heart, I cried, "But Daddy, I feel like I don't have my own country and I don't have my own culture. You're all the roots I have and if you were to remarry, I don't know what I would do." But I knew that this was his way to get his life back together and so I said, "Go ahead. I think it's a great idea." I could feel my father's pain when he said, "Loneliness kills." I didn't want him to be lonely anymore. He had found someone new for his life and I needed to let him go.

Once again, I plunged into my academics. I went to a graduate program in New York. I graduated with an M.B.A. in 1979 and headed for my first management consulting job in Washington D.C. "Here I come, world," I said. In Washington, I filled my life with long hours of work. When working long hours didn't fill my emptiness, I plunged into a relationship where I tried to be everything this man needed to get him to love me the way I needed to be loved. Then one day, he dropped me off at home and simply said, "It's over. I never want to see you again." I asked him, "What happened?" He said, "Nothing. I just woke up this morning and decided I don't love you anymore."

As I walked back to my apartment, his words opened up the wounds of the past. In the same way that my mother exited from my life, his sudden exit threw me into a tailspin. There was so much in life that I needed and so much I could not control. I found that when you cry out, "I really need you to stay," some people just walk away. I used to think that perhaps if someone really understood how much I needed them, they would stay. But I have learned that even when I am perfectly clear in expressing what I need, some people simply don't care. Other times, it's because they are in so much pain themselves that they have nothing left to give.

I remember just wanting the pain in my heart to stop. The week before, I had gone to see a doctor because my stomach was hurting. The doctor thought perhaps I had an ulcer and prescribed me some tranquilizers. In the aloneness in my apartment, I reached for the bottle of tranquilizers. I thought to take one pill to numb the pain I was feeling. Then I took another, and then another. All I wanted was for the pain to stop. Before I knew it, I had taken the whole bottle. I was not intentionally thinking about taking my own life. I just wanted the pain to stop.

I remember seeing the room spin and then I became unconscious. In God's mercy I woke up the next morning. The thought of not existing on earth anymore scared me. How could I have allowed anyone to cause me so much pain? How could I have allowed someone to trample on my heart? How could I have made excuses for him over and over again when I knew so well that some people will

use you for their purpose and then toss you away without
any hesitation?

I WAS LOOKING FOR A QUICK ANSWER

I DECIDED I HAD TO GET AWAY FROM THIS MAN WHO
had such a hold on my life. So, I accepted a job with
Exxon corporation in New Jersey. Here I was, a woman
of 24. I bought my first house. I worked for one of the
largest companies in the world. In all the ways that the
world defined success, I was a success. But deep inside, I
felt myself dying.

Then God planted another seed. I don't know how but
I stumbled into a little church in the suburbs. The pastor's
name was Phil and his wife was Mary. When they found
out that I was a single woman with no family in town,
they practically adopted me. We were so familiar that in
the middle of the day, when life got too much for me, I
would ring their door bell and crash on their couch.
While I was with them, once again, I was reminded of
Jesus and His love for me. And then I concluded, "Jesus,
you are fine for some people, but you are not enough for
me."

I didn't know then that God revealed Himself in the
Bible and that for all the power of God to be released in
me, then I had to know God's Word. Reading the Bible
took too much time. I was looking for a quick answer.

In 1980, Bob Carman transferred from Brussels,

Belgium to New Jersey. We dated for a period of six weeks and decided to get married. I was going to fill my emptiness with a Prince Charming and marriage. Bob was transferred back to Belgium in August and we were scheduled to be married in November. I remember Exxon coming in to pack my belongings and as I watched the moving van drive off to ship my belongings across the ocean, I said to myself, "What am I doing? I hardly know this man." As evidence of how well I knew him, Bob came back from Belgium three days before the wedding and he said to me, "Honey, why are we having our wedding at a Lutheran church?" I said, "That's because you're Lutheran." He said, "I'm not Lutheran. I thought it was because you were Lutheran." I said, "I'm not Lutheran." But we decided to proceed anyway because the pastor was so nice.

One day after our wedding, we flew to Brussels, Belgium and God allowed me to walk into a wilderness. Here I was, stripped of my work and my colleagues, all I had were the four walls around me and I crashed. Emotionally, I felt as if I was falling off a cliff and the pit was bottomless. My husband came home every night to find his wife sobbing hysterically. Out of desperation, he said, "Let's go to church" and God began to build our marriage upon Him, in a little missions church in Brussels, Belgium. I began to feel better and so I said, "Have thine own way, Lord. I will surrender my life to Jesus Christ" for this was a convenient time. I was sort of in-between jobs. So I said, "Here I am, God with all my talents and all my resources. I shall be a formidable force for your kingdom." And I was surprised that God was silent. So, out of my frustration, I said, "Fine, you don't want me. I'll go back to the corporate world."

In 1982, ten months into Belgium, Bob transferred back to New Jersey and I joined Booz, Allen and Hamilton, one of the top management consulting companies in the world. In three years time, I flew up the corporate ladder, from analyst, to senior analyst, to project manager, to being the manager of a new department. The same day I got my long sought-for appointment, Bob called to say, "You know that job in Houston, the one I said I would never get. I just got it." I worked late that night. When I came home, I asked him, "When does Exxon need to know?" He said, "Tomorrow." I told him, "Take it." He never said another word, perhaps for fear that I might change my mind. But, I knew that my long sought-after appointment didn't satisfy like I thought it would. At least Bob knew he would be happy in the new job in Houston. At least this way, one of us could be happy.

GOD TOUCHED MY LIFE IN THREE SIGNIFICANT AREAS

IN 1985, WE RELOCATED TO HOUSTON, TEXAS. I WENT back to work for Exxon out of a spouse relocation program. Then one day, out of sheer frustration from feeling an emptiness on the inside, I said, "I know what I'll do. I'll have a baby." In 1986, my first son, Robbie was born. I was so sure that in six weeks time, I would return to work but something happened that I didn't count on. Robbie had such a tug on my heart that I couldn't leave. I blamed my husband. I said, "It was your idea to breast-feed. I read somewhere that when you breastfeed, your body secretes these chemicals that make you extra mater-nal. That's why I'm this way." At the same time, I heard the familiar voice of Jesus from my childhood days, as clearly as if He were standing in this room. He said, "Follow me." "Follow you?" I said, "Are you kidding?" not knowing then that God kids not. So I proceeded to tell Him, as if He didn't know, "Oh, God, I'm not like other people. You see, I feel as if I don't have my own country and I don't have my own culture. My academics and my career, that's all I have. They are my roots, my hope…my God." God said, "That's why you must leave it." So, when in doubt, you punt for time. So I extended my maternity leave and extended my maternity leave. Eight months into my maternity leave, I called Exxon and I resigned.

I wish I could say that after that step of obedience, everything was fine but it wasn't. I walked into the great-est depression in my life. I was trained for corporate America and I had no idea what to do on the home front. So I decided, "How hard could this be? All I have to do is to transfer my management skills to running the home." So, I began to keep logs and logs of data on my baby. I knew when he slept, I knew when he woke, I wrote down every bowel movement. And then I began to plot that data in my computer, thinking that I could find some pattern to this baby, not knowing that babies have no pattern and once you figure it out, they will change it on you. I know now why God didn't send me any friends. I was totally neurotic. No one would have been edified by their friendship with me.

In the midst of my grasping for straws, God had a plan for my life and He was perfectly able to orchestrate events to walk me into that plan. In 1987, God in His mercy, began to weave the fragments of my life together to give me His dream for me. God touched my life in three significant areas.

God used my writing for His purpose. One year into motherhood, I said to God, "Please save my mind!" and God led me to writing. I wrote my first article and asked God to confirm that this was what He wanted me to do. A month later, I received a letter from the publisher of Home Life magazine wanting to buy my article. My first story printed under the title, "Mom for God's Glory". I was so excited, I said, "This is it!" and I began to write article after article. I have enough rejection letters to wallpaper a room. So I said, "God, I am so confused. I thought you wanted me to write. If this is what you want me to do, please show me one person who is edified by anything that I write." A few days later, I was walking down the hall of a church I was visiting and there was a surplus Home Life magazine that was tossed on a table. I picked it up and as I was skimming through the pages, my eyes landed on a familiar name. It was my name and the words read, "I wish to thank Anita Carman for her article, "Mom for God's Glory". I knew then that God had spoken and I didn't know when, and I didn't know how, but I knew that some day, somewhere, somehow, God would use my writing for His glory.

The second area God worked on was to create in me a servant's heart. Through my sons, God taught me humility before I could go in His name to serve His world. God humbled me through Robbie my older son and my younger son, Thomas, who was born 19 months later. There would be no more designer clothes. There would be no more limousine pickups. Instead, I have spit running down my back. I have ice cream in my hair. I have diarrhea smeared all over my Sunday clothes. I find myself running frantically in a mall because this baby who just nursed five minutes ago decides that he is starving to death. So I am scrambling to find a private place to nurse him. Of course, there is no such place. So I find myself hiding in a Sears bathroom, sitting on the commode, and while he is gurgling away, I stare blankly at the bathroom door in front of me and at my tennis shoes and I say, "Oh, you've come a long way, baby. If only the partners of my firm could see me now."

I remember during this time, I went to a church retreat workshop on motherhood. It was one of those workshops where people went around the circle sharing their experiences. The question was "What do you think of motherhood?" The first person said, "Motherhood is a dream come true." The second person said, "Motherhood is a fairytale." The third person said, "Motherhood is the best thing that ever happened to me." When it came to my turn, I thought, "Should I lie?" But it didn't seem right to do so at a church retreat. So I said, "Motherhood was like death because one of us had to die so the other could live. One of us had to lay down our personal ambitions and needs to take care of the needs of the other." Well, you could have heard a pin drop. No one said anything and then everyone said, "Oh, it was the pits! I hated those 2 a.m. feedings. I couldn't even get away to go to the bathroom. I always had this permanent appendage clinging on me." Then I learned something. I learned that women lie. And women put other women on guilt trips. And the older ones have this attitude, "Well, if I suffered, then you must suffer too."

Both of my sons will soon be out of the nest. They are so good to their mother and so good for their mother. They have the analytical logical mind of their father. I remember one day I had disciplined Robbie for an incident, he said to me, "Mother, I feel the punishment you gave me is disproportional to my wrong behavior. Did something happen today to get you upset?" He then goes down the list, "Did someone call? Did you hear a song that reminded you of your past? What happened today while I was at school?" I could hear the concern in his voice and the way he was trying to analyze the situation to help me through my emotions. At another time, I remember being so upset with Thomas that I said, "Go to your room. No more computers. No more games." His brother jumped in and said, "And no more food!" Thomas stormed up the stairs. Then within minutes, he was singing as he skipped down the stairs. He sang, "I believe...I believe...Jesus loves me..." Then he proclaimed loudly, "Jesus loves me this I know. You can take away my computer, you can take away my games, you can take away my food, but you can't take away the fact that Jesus died on the cross for me!" I started laughing. My kids have a great way to help their mother lighten up. Thomas often says to me, "Mother, because your life was hard, I feel my role in life is to be happy. Aren't you glad that your kids are happy?" When I am overworked and forget details, my sons never accuse me or blame me. Instead, I remember Thomas saying, "The reason why Mommy calls me Darling is because she can't remember my name!" Through my sons, I have learned that I cannot erase some of the sadness of the past. There are years the locusts have eaten that I cannot restore. However, I can affect the future for the next generation.

The third area God worked on was in giving me a foundation in His Word. Kathy, my sister-in-law said, "Why don't you join a bible study?" "A bible study?" I said. "What do I need a bible study for?" She directed me to Bible Study Fellowship. I went to Bible Study Fellowship (BSF) so I could have someone to go to lunch with. When I went to the introduction class, I found out that BSF was a six-year program. I thought anyone who signed up for a six-year bible study needed to get a life. I was surprised when I signed up. God sent me such a wonderful leader who called me every week. Her name was Alice Peacock. I said to Alice, "It's not working. I don't feel stronger." She said, "Oh, God has such treasures for you. Come back, just one more week." Out of love for Alice, I returned. Then I signed up the next year and the next, till I finally graduated from Bible Study Fellowship.

PICK UP YOUR MAT AND WALK

THE SAME TIME I WAS IN BIBLE STUDY FELLOWSHIP, I was in Beth Moore's Sunday School class. Unbeknownst to me, there was a battle for my life. As I inhaled God's Word day and night, I want you to know that God won. God is true to His Word. He said you will know the truth and the truth will set you free. Three years into bible study, I was in the gospel of John, reading about the man who had been crippled for 38 years. In John 5:6-11, the Apostle John tells the story: When Jesus saw him lying there and learned that he had been in this condition for a long time, he asked him, "Do you want to get well?" "Sir," the invalid replied, "I have no one to help me into the pool when the water is stirred. While I am trying to get in, someone else goes down ahead of me." Then Jesus said to him, "Get up! Pick up your mat and walk." At once the man was cured; he picked up his mat and walked.

As I read these words, God opened my eyes to see my

own condition. He impressed on my heart these words, "You are like this man. The same way he said he had no man to help him get to the water, you have been saying, 'Oh Jesus, if only…If only I had a friend, if only I had the right degree, if only I had the right job, if only I lived in the right city, if only I had my Prince Charming, if only I had children, if only I had the right house, then I would be whole.'" And Jesus said, "Just as I said to the crippled man I am saying to you that you don't need anything or anyone else but me. You rise up and walk."

That same night, I was reading in Luke 13 about the woman who was bent down with an affliction for eighteen years and I thought, "That's about the amount of time since my mother's death." And God said to the woman, "You are healed of your affliction" and God's Word said, "Immediately she was made well."

And that was exactly what happened to me. I woke up the next morning looking for my pain but instead, I found a song in my heart.

THERE COMES A DECISION POINT WHEN YOU MUST CHOOSE

WHEN YOUR HEART WILL NOT LET GO OF DREAMS from your past, remember that new beginnings begin in you. God is perfectly able to orchestrate events to walk you into His perfect plan for your life. But there will come a decision point when you must choose to step into

God's plan.

So often, when I hear testimonies I want to know, "And then what happened?" So, I'm here to tell you what happened. Nothing happened for about two years. I returned to the cocoon of my isolation and then one day, in August of 1991, I received a phone call from my Sunday School teacher, Beth Moore, asking me to teach her class. At the time, Beth had a class of 300 women. I was thinking, "Why did she single me out?" So, I said, "From all the people in the class, what made you call me?" She said, "God placed your name on my heart." That week, I was in a bible study where the teacher pointed out that Samuel invited Saul to be King. Her point was, "When someone filled with God's Spirit invites you to do something, take it seriously." So, on faith, I taught Beth's class.

Donna Lewis, a leader in Beth's class, who was planning a retreat, called me up the next week to ask if I could speak at the retreat. October 1991 was my first retreat. Beth Moore was in the audience and she came up to me and said, "Anita, I don't know how to tell you this but I believe God has called you to be a speaker." I thought, "That can't be true. I've told them everything that I know. There's nothing left to say." But if God had called me to be a speaker, I decided I had better be prepared. So I enrolled at the Houston extension campus of Dallas Theological Seminary.

When different churches and denominations invited me to speak, I said to God, "Am I a speaker?" He said,

"You are today but who knows about tomorrow?" God's style bothered me. I found Him to be totally unpredictable. Why couldn't He give me a five-year business plan?

Since then, I have learned that the safest place to be is in the center of God's will. I have learned that I don't need to know about tomorrow because tomorrow will take care of itself. What I need to do is to focus on my choices for today. God is the one who will connect the dots. Can I simply pray, "Give us this day our daily bread" and can I simply give Him today and let Him plan my tomorrows?

4

How Will Your Story End?

I REMEMBER WHEN IT WAS TIME TO LEAVE MY COUNTRY, I said to my Dad, "I don't have to go." Deep in his heart, he preferred for me to stay because he had just lost my mother and he was dreading the loss of his two daughters. He did not want to return from the airport to an empty house. But he said to me, "Don't be silly. You must go."

There are times in our lives when new beginnings catch us off-guard. When the door of opportunity opens it is so much easier to cling to what is familiar than to walk into the unknown. Today, my Dad lives in Houston, Texas. He volunteers at Inspire Women every week. What if he hadn't had the courage to let me go? What if I didn't have the courage to leave?

"YOU HAVE THE CLOAK, JUST DIP IT IN THE WATER!"

PERSONALLY, I NEVER FELT READY FOR NEW BEGINNINGS because the greatest emotional need in my life was for roots. When I was in Beth Moore's class, I felt safe under the umbrella of her protection. I always saw Beth as being stronger and more resilient than I was. She seemed to bounce back quickly when unjustly criticized. I, on the other hand, when criticized, would be flat on my back for days trying to find the strength to get up off the ground. My emotional reservoir was pitifully close to empty. I needed the blessing of others because I wanted to fit into a community. God had to get rid of my weakness because it would limit me and become a stumbling block to where He wanted to take me. God had to wean me off the relationships I depended on so I could find strength in experiencing His sufficiency.

When Beth first invited me to teach her class, my stomach cramped for days. Never once did I ever sit in the audience thinking I should be on the platform. When Beth said to me, "If it's not me, then it's you," I wanted to be the best substitute teacher she ever had. But one day, Beth said to me, "Anita, I believe your ministry is outside of my class." When I found myself running back to her for help, she said, "Anita, you seem to think you need something from me. I want you to know you don't need anything from me. You have the cloak, just dip it in the water." Those words should have caused me to celebrate. Instead I wept for days. I didn't want to have the cloak. I wanted to be her substitute and to be part of her family.

One Sunday, Beth taught a lesson on Elijah and Elisha and handed me an outline on which she wrote, "This lesson is dedicated to you." I cherished her note like an item in a baby's scrap book. I tried to appear independent but leaving her class broke my heart. I did not understand why God's calling in our lives required so many good-byes. Beth called me and left a message on my answering machine the day I left her class. She said, "Anita Carman, today I welcome you as an equal."

GOD WOULD NOT BE IMPRISONED BY MY PAST EMOTIONAL BAGGAGE!

WHEN I WENT TO DALLAS THEOLOGICAL SEMINARY, my first professor was Dr. William Boyd, who also happened to be the President of the College of Biblical Studies. Emotionally, I felt like a scared little bird that had been pushed out of the nest. I was sure I was going to die in the wilderness. So I transferred my dependence from Beth to Dr. Boyd. I found security in his class. I only had Dr. Boyd for one class but he made quite an impression on me. He taught me that the goal of our instruction was love. So from his class, I tried to soak in every word all the professors were teaching me so I could express God's heart with greater love to those around me.

I did not see Dr. Boyd for some time after my first class. Then two years later, to my surprise, I received a phone call from Dr. Boyd. He said, "Anita, I would like an appointment with you." I said, "What for?" He said, "I would like to talk to you about a job."

What he didn't know was that I had planned on returning to corporate America. I convinced myself that God had only been testing me to see if I would leave my career but that now, He was giving me permission to return to my corporate career. So, I interviewed for a job as a management consultant. I had gone through several levels of interviews. As I advanced to the next level, I celebrated it as God's green light. I was finally offered the job with a great salary and a bonus for performance. All looked wonderful till the company called to tell me the Vice President had resigned and had taken half the clientele. Therefore, the company did not need my services anymore.

I was confused. How could so many green lights have ended in a dead end? I felt like God had dangled a carrot in front of me only to take it away. I went to God and asked Him why He allowed so many green lights only to slam the door in my face. He told me that He wanted me to see that if I wanted to return to corporate America, I still had the skills to do so. He didn't want me serving Him because I had no other option. But He was asking me once again if I would use my life to build an eternal kingdom. I learned that God does not chatter. He speaks His will and leaves things alone. I am the one who continues to question what I heard. I am the one who tires myself out by going back and forth in God's marching orders.

I really wasn't sure what using my life to build an eternal kingdom meant. Did it mean going to work for a nonprofit organization? So I started to make a list of the kinds of non-profit organizations I would want to work for. At the time, my classes at Dallas Theological Seminary met on the campus of the College of Biblical Studies (CBS). I noticed on the campus that the students attending CBS were mostly minorities. I knew God wanted worship from every tribe and nation. I knew God's heart sang when His sons and daughters from every ethnicity gathered every evening and weekend to study His Word. I wanted to be where God's heart was rejoicing. So I said to God, "If I had my choice, I would work for the College of Biblical Studies."

Three days later, Dr. Boyd was on the phone offering me a job when I had not contacted him or inquired about any job opening. I was curious why Dr. Boyd decided to call me since I had not spoken to him for quite a while. He said something about keeping my homework assignment in his files. He said it was the best work he had seen in his twenty five years of teaching. I think my homework must have fallen out of his files on a day that He was asking God who he needed to invite to join him in ministry. I wasn't sure why he felt that what I did in the classroom equaled transferable skills for what he needed me to do at the college. Actually, I wasn't quite sure what he wanted me to do. It seemed to be a little of teaching and reaching women and building relationships and recruiting and encouraging those with financial ability to give to the college. But whatever the job description was, I was sure God had opened the door and I was to walk through it.

Dr. Boyd invited me to join him at the College of Biblical Studies to be their Director of Women's Ministry.

I called Pastor David Self from my home church and asked his counsel. He told me to always walk through the door that will help me reach more people with God's Word. He told me to just do the next right thing and to allow God to connect the dots. He told me not to worry about what an assignment will lead to. Just choose the next open door that will bless the most people. It was by following this counsel that I learned to respond to every assignment Dr. Boyd gave me as God's open door to stretch me in a different direction. In the five years at the College, I had other titles added to me. I ended up being Director of Women's Ministry, Vice President of Special Programs and Special Assistant to the President.

While at the college, someone who worked in the development office told me she recognized that the address for a monthly donation we were receiving was coming from someone who lived in the low income government housing. She was sure there was a story behind why this person was sending us a regular monthly donation of $25. I found out that the woman had been a student at the College. She had dropped out of her classes because she could not afford the tuition. She was sending us $25 a month hoping that her contribution would help someone else stay in school. I went to ask Dr. Boyd if we could offer her a scholarship. He told me I could offer this woman a scholarship if I raised it.

That week, I stumbled into a biography on the founder of a ministry that addresses world hunger. I read that he was in India when he found a little girl in the streets. He carried her to the orphanage and a nun who opened the door said, "We're full." He said, "It's just one more." She answered, "It's always just one more." She put the girl in his arms and said, "You feed her." That incident was the catalyst to his efforts to birth a ministry to feed the hungry.

Through this story, I heard the Lord say to me, "I am putting spiritual children in your arms. Feed my sheep." I had no idea how I would raise scholarship funds. The Lord told me to pick up the phone and impressed a name on my heart. I dialed the number and the person I was calling said, "I am inundated with bills." Then she said, "I've been unemployed for eighteen months. Do you think I should go back to work?" I thought to myself, "Lord, this can't be the person!" He said, "Ask her." So I said, "I know this may not be a good time but I just wonder if God might be inviting you to rise above your own needs to respond to the need of a sister in Christ?" I asked if she would sponsor a scholarship.

There was silence on the phone. I could hear my own heart beating. Then I realized that it was not my heart beating, it was God's heart that was beating. He was the one who had asked. He was simply using my mouth and He was waiting for an answer. Then from the other side of the line came this response, "I would be happy to do it." After that first scholarship, word got out and other students who needed help started coming. Miraculously, God would help me to raise the funds to keep them in school. I did not realize God was laying the foundation for the scholarship program of Inspire Women.

In 2001, Dr. Boyd and the leaders of CBS decided they wanted to do a citywide women's conference. My thoughts were, "If we are to do a women's conference, we should do one that reflects the multi-ethnic color of the city." My next thoughts were, "I've never even organized a lunch for 5 people so, I can't possibly be the one for the assignment." Against that inside voice that said, "You have no connections. You can't possibly rally the city in a multi-ethnic vision" was the voice of God who said, "You are the daughter of a King. I am your connection. Go in my name and I will go before you." I was grateful for my co-laborers Gene Tow and Eulalia King who helped me with the details of a conference.

From the very beginning, God's hand was on Inspire. I asked the Lord for a database to track the registrations from a citywide conference. Then, in walked Sheryll Roberson who offered to volunteer her time. When I asked her what her skills were, she said, "I work as a computer programmer and I have a Masters in Computer Science."

At the first time event in 2001, the Inspire Women's Conference drew nearly 3000 women from over 650 different churches, of which 40% were minorities. When I reflect on the first Inspire Women's Conference, I marvel at the incredible women God raised up as role models of His multi-ethnic vision. Instead of having their own platform in the workshops, local leaders of different ethnicities teamed up to co-teach a workshop (see Appendix, p.180-181 Leaders Who Shared). Because the leaders united, their audiences united. But, best of all, in my heart I could hear God singing from the throne room of heaven. The names of the leaders in our city who joined God in His multi-ethnic vision at the Inspire Women's Conference since 2001 are listed in the appendix. I believe their names have been written in God's Hall of Fame (see Appendix, p.179-178 Leaders).

The citywide conference was quite a production. It took every ounce of energy to rally every living soul to help in some way. I remember on the day of the conference all the volunteers were in place early in the morning. Then, it was as if someone opened the floodgates and one after another the cars started to roll in. When the women started walking in, we could see them coming towards the glass doors of the front entrance. They appeared like an avalanche descending on us. I still remember the look on the faces of the volunteers. Some of them literally turned white. For one split second, everyone froze and just stared at the scene. And then without a word, everyone went into action and the volunteers did whatever they could to take care of the crowd.

As I reflect on the ministry of Inspire Women, I see God's mercy in casting a wide net into the city to search for His gems who desire to connect their lives with His purpose (see Appendix, p.176 Reach). For those who need additional training to step into God's calling for their lives but do not have the funds for training, Inspire Women then funds scholarships to train women for ministry. The conference is produced back to back with an awards luncheon which serves as our major fund raiser.

In 2003, the College of Biblical Studies was focusing its efforts in a capital campaign and could no longer channel its resources into producing a women's event. I was given the option to stay to help with the capital campaign and with other programs in the school but to shut down Inspire. I believe Dr. Boyd was sensitive to the fact that God had used me to birth Inspire and he had witnessed what God had done through Inspire in the lives of the women. In his kindness, Dr. Boyd offered me the option to take Inspire with his blessings and to go. I asked, "What exactly does that mean?" He said, "Take the mailing list, take the logo and see what you can do with it." Even as Dr. Boyd said these words, I knew it broke his heart. What he didn't realize was how much I dreaded the idea of leaving.

I had known for several months that, as long as Inspire was under the umbrella of the College, it could not reach its potential as a women's ministry. I had discussed my observations with several trusted leaders at the College and they all agreed that Inspire needed to separate and to develop its own identity. One leader said, "You can bless more students than just those at the College of Biblical Studies. You can help those going for training in other institutions. It will serve the kingdom better if Inspire became an independent non-profit organization." No matter how many times I talked through the reasons for separating, the idea of letting go of the students at the

College I had grown to love, was heart wrenching to me. Moreover, I wanted to cling to Dr. Boyd as my spiritual father. I reminded God, "I've always needed a place to belong. This separation is not good for me emotionally." But God would not be imprisoned by my past emotional baggage.

When Dr. Boyd wrote the letter to announce my departure, I knew there was no turning back. As I read and re-read this letter, I could not believe that this was happening. Dr. Boyd began his letter with the following paragraphs:

> *I'll never forget how painful it was to take my daughters to college. Their absence was painful—but I knew it was right. They had matured and grown up, and now they were ready for a new challenge.*
>
> *Anita Carman is almost like my daughter. She took her first seminary class from me when I was an adjunct professor for Dallas Theological Seminary. Then she came to CBS to help us build the largest multi-ethnic Bible College in North America.*
>
> *In the process, Anita designed the Inspire! Women's Ministry. It truly is a reflection of the gifts that God has given her to use in building His kingdom. She has the inordinate ability to ignite a sleeping sister—to literally inspire women to see themselves as God designed them and to mobilize women as a united force for God's kingdom. Given the requests from women for Inspire to develop into ongoing programs throughout the year to network women across ethnicities for mutual encouragement and service, Inspire has the potential to be a ministry all by itself. As we at CBS watched God bless Inspire, it has become apparent that God is calling Anita to step out and fly on her own. Like leaving my daughter at college, it is painful, but in our hearts, we believe this move best serves the Kingdom of God.*

As I read the letter, I wanted to tear it up and to tell Dr. Boyd not to send it out. I wanted to say, "Let's just forget this whole thing. Let's just scrap Inspire and I'll stay here and build the College with you." But I knew if I stayed, I would never discover where God could take Inspire. I would always regret "what could have been." Something inside me felt that Inspire had the potential to become this great engine to find God's gems in our city and to train women in the programs that best fit their calling. Something inside me felt that what God was doing for the women in Houston would one day be replicated in every major city throughout the country. What was standing between me and God's vision was me. Would I walk away from what was tangible and visible to believe in the vision God had entrusted to me?

"ARE YOU MORE IMPRESSED WITH A BUILDING THAN YOU ARE WITH ME?"

ON MAY 1 OF 2003, I DROVE AWAY FROM THE College of Biblical Studies with all my boxes in my car, zero in the bank, no office space and no infrastructure but God's vision for Inspire to invest in the potential of the women of the city for His service was clear. How the vision would be implemented, I had no idea. All I had was a logo and a mailing list and the conference and luncheon were scheduled to be produced in six month's time, in November 2003. Alberta Harris who had experience working for Promise Keepers offered me her assistance. While I labored to shape the organization, she took over the administrative and production details. Her friendship encouraged me greatly.

As I was driving away from the college, I had tears streaming down my face. As I looked at the building in my rear mirror, I heard God say, "Anita, are you more impressed with a building than you are with me?" I said to God, "Yes I am! There is a building there. There is a desk. There is a receptionist. You are a Spirit!" Then God said, "Now you will see I am more real than all that you see around you!"

The same month I drove away from the College of Biblical Studies, I was scheduled to go to Dallas Theological Seminary in Dallas, Texas for my graduation. At first, I did not plan to attend my graduation because I felt my life was in a major upheaval. Several people called to ask if I would be going. I wasn't sure why they were so concerned about my being at the graduation. I finally decided to go because my father was almost eighty and he had never seen me graduate. When I received my bachelor's and my master's degrees, he could not afford the airplane ticket to be there. So, here I was getting another Master's degree from seminary and I thought perhaps he would be excited to watch me walk down the aisle to get my diploma. When I arrived at the graduation ceremony, I realized why several people were trying to get me to attend. They knew that I had won an award and they wanted to be sure I was present to receive it. I received Dallas Theological Seminary's award for the top student with the best academic achievement. When I received my award, all I could think of was, "God, you are so good. The very timing of this is your way to tell me that your hands are on my life. You are affirming your calling through this award. You are reminding me that you have prepared me before sending me into the world with your mission."

When I returned to Houston after the fanfare at the graduation, I walked back into a vacuum. The question that I asked every morning was, "God, now what?" Then I watched God hand me a brick, one brick at a time. I received an audio teaching tape from Cindy Walker, one of the workshop speakers I had invited to speak at the 2003 Inspire women's conference. On it, she said, "I ran into my friend Dougal Cameron." Dougal was the name someone had given me. I knew that he owned buildings and perhaps he might have some office space for me. I asked Cindy how well she knew Dougal. She said, "I'm best friends with his wife." I asked her, "Would you mind calling his wife on behalf of Inspire Women? We really need office space." When Cindy called Cathy Cameron she said, "I know Anita Carman. She does not remember me but I met her in 1991 when she spoke at the Texas Women's Retreat. I had overfilled my table and I was put at the speaker's table next to her." Cathy felt that God had woven our lives back together. Cindy called me to say, "Cathy said to call her husband and he'll take care of you." Three weeks into May, Inspire Women moved into over 2,000 square feet of donated space.

As soon as we moved in, I said to the Lord, "We have no furniture." One morning, through the connections of Lesha Elsenbrook, I received a phone call. The voice on the other side of the line said, "Anita Carman? Inspire Women?" I said, "Yes." The voice said, "This is Jody Hoffer of Hoffer Furniture. I heard you needed furniture. I've talked to my manager. Come in and pick out what you need." Through Hoffer Furniture, Inspire Women was furnished with credenzas and bookshelves. That same weekend, I walked into Office Depot and they had their desks for sale. The strangest thing was, the manufacturer was offering a rebate. The desk was marked down to $49 and the rebate was for $50. Could it be that we would get back $1 for each desk we bought?

Donna Fujimoto Cole, the CEO of Cole Chemical offered me a beautiful conference table which we moved to the office. I remember walking in and thinking, "Lord, we have no chairs." The next day I walked in and there were beautiful maroon padded chairs around the table. Where did the chairs come from? I found out that the maintenance crew of the building noticed we didn't have chairs for our conference table. So, they scoured the building asking the tenants to return the chairs they had borrowed and put all the chairs around our conference table.

Meredith Iler gave Inspire a couch and armchair. Karen McCord became our girl Friday. In the heat of the summer, she arranged pickup trucks and physically moved heavy pieces of furniture into our space. None of the furniture in the office matched because the items came from different sources. In a way, the office looked like a garage sale. But the wonderful thing was, everywhere I turned I saw an item that reminded me of a friend who proved their love for the women of the city through their support and donation to the ministry. I also learned how very little we needed when our priority is to do ministry. As long as the furniture was functional, what difference did it make that nothing matched?

As soon as we were furnished, I said to the Lord, "We have no computers." Through a contact with Barbara Harris Curtis, Terence Drew who refurbished computers showed up on our premises and gave us our computers. In addition, Pastor Gusta Booker from Greater St. Matthew Church delivered a brand new computer to my home. Mike Taylor showed up to network all the computers together and to help us with our telephone lines.

When I went to speak at a women's fundraiser at Greater St. Matthew Church, the pastor's wife, Theola Booker, said to the women, "I know this was supposed to be our fund raiser but I feel strongly led to take up a love offering for Inspire Women." I was asked to stand in the front of the church with a fish basket. Each woman in the church came down the aisle and sowed a financial seed into the basket. I was totally humbled to stand before my sisters in Christ to receive a gift from their heart to the women of the city.

Pastor Remus Wright of the Fountain of Praise Church

sent word to me that the space at his church would always be available to Inspire Women. I finally took him up on his offer to have the Inspire 2005 conference at his church. Dr. David Self, William Taylor, Barbara Evans, and Carolyn O'Neal from Houston's First Baptist Church were always available to offer counsel and support. They said, "We're here for you!" With the church's blessing, Scott Reavis, the graphics artist from the church donated his graphics design services. Pastor Leonard Barksdale from Fifth Ward Missionary Baptist Church and Pastor Johnnie Lee of Victory in Jesus Evangelistic Center gave sacrificially to Inspire on a monthly basis to encourage us. Pastor Paul Cannings of Living Word Fellowship told his church staff, "I don't ever want Inspire Women to wait for their monthly check. I want it to be the first check to go out every month."

To handle the volume of phone calls that come in during the time of the conference, I knew Inspire Women would need a phone system. I'm not even sure how Steve Stockwill of The Via Group entered into God's script. It was as if God raised up different personalities and companies in His perfect timing to do the next thing that needed to be done. Before long, I realized that Inspire Women was God's dream and I was simply going along for the ride. Steve said, "Your problem is, you are a huge company with a large customer base. But you are also a small company because you have no money." He told me about a system he had in his warehouse that could be modified to suit our needs. I asked him how much the system was.

He said it would run between $25,000-$30,000. I told him we didn't have that kind of money. He said, "Let me talk to my boss." He came back to say, "We would be happy to donate the system to you." I asked him, "Can you donate the installation as well?" He said, "We would be happy to donate the installation as well."

"YOU KNOW WHO YOUR REAL FRIENDS ARE WHEN YOU NEED A BOWL OF RICE!"

FRANCIE WILLIS HAD ALREADY ACCEPTED TO BE THE chair of the Inspire Women's Luncheon for November 2003 but I had no idea if she would back out, now that I was no longer with the College of Biblical Studies. When I went in to see her, she said, "What is this? Do I hear fear in your voice? We'll have none of that. Now that you are no longer with the College, we'll take the luncheon to the next level." I wasn't sure how to respond. I just wanted to fall at her feet and kiss them. I was reminded of what my mother once told me, "You know who your real friends are when you need a bowl of rice." I saw that Francie Willis, the CEO of the Urban Retreat had a life mission of replenishment. Not only was her mission to replenish those who were physically in need of refreshment but her heart was to replenish those who needed spiritual renewal. Any time we surfaced a need, Francie's favorite answer was, "I'll take care of it."

Francie Willis went down in God's spiritual journal as taking the luncheon to the next level. But, both she and I knew that we were building on the efforts of the previous luncheon chairs who lent us their influence. I will forever be grateful to Elizabeth Wareing who birthed the first Inspire Women's Luncheon in November of 2001. With Beth Lee as her assistant, she guided me ever so patiently. Never once did she grow impatient with me. She literally took me by the hand and led me one day at a time. Our luncheon chairs and honorees for our other years are listed in the appendix. When I look at this list, it shows me that God's Holy Spirit is the one who is rallying our city. I am humbled to be in the presence of those God entrusted with greatness and who, in their humility and obedience, so freely give themselves away in service.

I DIDN'T WANT TO GO DOWN IN SPIRITUAL HISTORY AS BEING AFRAID

A CRITICAL ELEMENT THAT HAD TO HAPPEN AFTER Inspire Women separated as an independent non-profit organization was to round up the financial support. Every morning, God instructed me who to call, where to go, and what to ask for. There were times when I found myself saying, "Lord, are you sure you want me to just go in and ask for that?" After a while, I didn't care anymore how absurd the request sounded. I settled in my mind that Noah built an ark when there was no rain. In the same way, God had me on an assignment where I was simply to do whatever He told me to do. I felt like I was going through some kind of revolving door where we only had so much time to get through or else lose all momentum.

On many days, I felt afraid but I didn't want to go down in spiritual history as being afraid. My stomach cramped before I picked up a phone to call a prospective supporter but I forced myself to call anyway. Then the thought hit me, "Would I make a fool of myself and take a chance for God?" People take chances for business all the time. So what's so bad about taking a chance for God? Why is it that when it comes to God, we want a 100% guarantee? Besides, even if someone laughs at my persistence behind my back, what's so bad about standing in front of Jesus one day and saying "I chose to look like a total fool for you"?

God, in His mercy, put Donna Fujimoto Cole in my life. She was an Asian woman CEO with a compassionate heart for her community. Though we did not know each other that well, I trusted Donna with our need and asked if she would underwrite the conference. Donna told me later she had never committed that much money to a ministry before. She said, "It was a miracle that I said yes." Donna's generous pledge gave Inspire Women the assurance that our basic costs for the conference would be taken care of. She has remained a great mentor in my life.

When I had the chance to meet Linda Dunham for lunch, I could not believe I was sitting across the table from her. She was one of the kindest and gentlest persons

I had ever met. She reminded me of my friend Doris Morris. Doris is now with the Lord but I will never forget her friendship. I was a substitute teacher in Doris' Sunday School class. Doris saw right away that I was feeling inadequate in God's calling. So, she took it upon herself to encourage me by introducing me to her friends and making sure that everyone knew that she loved me and supported me in my efforts. Mary Ann Belin was another sister in Christ who took the time to have lunch with me and to encourage me. She had headed women's ministry at Second Baptist Church for many years and I immediately sensed her love for what Inspire Women was doing for the women of our city. Through Linda Duham, Doris Morris, and Mary Ann Belin, I saw great women of God in whom He could entrust His resources. They were always gracious and kind. In spite of their very busy schedules and the many demands on their lives, they blessed people wherever they went. They truly exhibited the heart and mercy of Jesus. Because of the cash flow needs at Inspire Women, the Dunham's made sure we received a check right away. Their kindness refreshed our spirit and tied us over till other checks came in.

When I began selling tables for the fundraiser luncheon, I was so new in understanding the workings of a non-profit organization that I did not know there was a difference between being approved by the IRS as a non-profit organization and getting a 501(c)3 status. Our CPA, Byron Ubernosky who had donated all his time, said to me, "You did know that your supporters cannot deduct their donation unless you are a 501(c)3 organization, didn't you?" Well, actually, I didn't know that. I was beside myself. How could I with integrity sell tables at the $5,000, $10,000, $25,000, $45,000 level and not have it be tax deductible? I asked Byron, "How long does it take to get 501(c)3 status?" He said, "We already submitted all the paperwork but it will take at least three to four months." I told him, "We don't have three to four months. We need to be selling the tables today."

I went to God and I said, "Father, if this ministry is from you, I ask you to give us our 501(c)3 status today. I ask that when I go to the mailbox, the letter from the IRS will be there." I went to my mailbox and there was the letter. Twenty nine days from the day we filed, Inspire Women was granted its 501(c)3 status. I called Byron and told him. He said, "In my twenty five years of service, I have never seen anyone approved in 29 days!" I casually told this story to a friend who once worked at the IRS. Her eyes widened as big as saucers. She said, "I hope you realize that what happened does not happen. I know because I used to be the one who approved organizations who apply for 501(c)3 status. I hope this sign will help you to never doubt God's hand on Inspire Women."

God continued to provide affirmation after affirmation. When the first mailing was ready to go out, I needed funds to pay the bill. One of our volunteers, Carl Grijalba asked me how much I needed. I said, "$3,500." He said he would give me the check. Then I found out the bill was for $5,000 but I didn't have the heart to tell Carl.

I was at church when he handed me his check and I stuck it in my Bible. When I got home and looked at it, the check was made out for $5,000. How did he know? I asked him why he made the check out for more than I had told him. He said he didn't know why. All he knew was, when he was making out the check, God told him to make it out for $5,000. Oh, how God's work advances on earth when we simply listen to the prompting of God's Spirit!

Roy Urrego designed the Inspire Women's website. I don't know if he ever realized how much it helped me to see that we had a website. In the days when we began with so little, having a website put in tangible form the vision God was birthing. Lee Bouldin designed the first Inspire Women stationery and business cards as a surprise gift. Bruce Munstermann of the radio station KHCB (Keeping Him Close By on FM 105.7) extended his hand of friendship by giving Inspire Women radio time on the station. His was a familiar voice on the radio and he lent Inspire Women his influence by introducing my teaching tapes with his voice. Martin and Ginger Gaston who own ENG Image made the commitment to walk in faith with Inspire Women. They travel all around town to shoot video footage to produce Inspire Women DVDs to capture the highlights of our ministry. Chan Do who owns Machan Design and Linda Huang, who was a Director of Marketing in a previous career, offered Inspire Women ongoing graphics design and marketing services on a donated basis. Tad Molloy of Printing-X-Press shares our vision to rally the city to raise an endowment for biblical

training and donates much of our printing to help us min-
imize our costs. Rozie Curtis from Theater Under the
Stars directs the programs at our events and oversees the
production of dramatic skits. It was clear that God had
separated the top in their fields to support the women of
the city.

As the Apostle Paul said in Hebrews 11:32, "And what
more shall I say? I do not have time to tell about Gideon,
Barak, Samson, Jephthah, David, Samuel and the
prophets", I praise God for the ministries, individuals and
vendors He raised up to encourage Inspire Women with
their generous donated services and time. Oh, how grateful I was for encouraging friends such as: Helen Perry and
Jeanette Burrell, who were always so willing to say "I'll
help you any way I can. Just call me!"; Deborah Clifton,
whose favorite words were "This is awesome!"; Cheryl
Thompson-Draper, who so often affirmed "I'm so proud
of you!"; and, Joanie Haley of the McNair Foundation,
who consistently blessed me with her words "Inspire
Women is doing an excellent job!". For a more complete
list of those God drew to rally behind me and His vision,
please refer to the Appendix, page 177-183. If I left anyone out, I beg your forgiveness. God knows the part you
played in His vision for His daughters and He has put you
in His Hall of Fame.

GOD WAS SENDING A STRONG MESSAGE TO THE CITY...

WHAT WOULD HAPPEN IF WOMEN CALLED BY GOD had the training to go anywhere in their community and in the world to establish training centers and various ministries? As more women answered God's call for service, the need for funds for biblical training increased. In 2005, God brought Cindy Crane Garbs, Bonnie Likover and Cindy Walker as co-chairs of the Inspire Women's Luncheon to rally even greater support to invest in women for biblical training. Because the luncheon drew supporters from those with influence and financial capability, the sellout of the luncheon sent a bold message to the city that God's leaders were voting to build a community grounded in His Word. Moreover, having adequate funds to train women in the programs that best prepared them for their calling resulted in services that met the need in the community such as programs to reach at-risk youth, children from abuse backgrounds, women in transition, etc. Instead of limiting a woman to one particular training institution, Inspire Women begins with God's dreams in women for ministry and matches her needs with the best program in town, ranging from a certificate level to a Master's degree level.

National leaders supported Inspire Women with their friendship. Jerry Shirer, the husband of Priscilla Evans said to me, "Anita, Priscilla will waive her honorarium to

speak at Inspire. We will walk in faith with you."
Priscilla's father, Dr. Tony Evans gave Inspire Women the
blessing to use an endorsement that read, "Anita Carman
moves at Spirit compelled speed with a contagious energy to expand God's kingdom on earth. I commend the
marvelous ministry of Inspire Women to train all God's
daughters in the biblical programs that best fit their calling." Beth Moore's office gave Inspire Women the blessing to use her endorsement: "Anita Carman is brilliant. I
am thrilled about her ministry. She has substitute taught
for me in Sunday School and at retreats. I trust her teaching totally." Jill Briscoe made herself available for the
conference and for an ongoing email relationship where
she offered her support and counsel. Kay Arthur invited
Inspire Women to visit her in her headquarters to discuss
the opportunities for a strategic partnership.

Visionary leaders who saw what God was doing
through Inspire Women to bless the women of the city
offered to hold brunches and receptions to introduce their
friends to be part of God's growing spiritual women's
movement. They were excited that God picked Houston
and that one day, other cities throughout the nation will
follow our example to bless the women of their own city.
Among those who offered their homes to rally their
friends included Debra Paxton, Uldine Bisagno, Julie
Jordan, Linda Dewhurst, Donna Bahoric, Cindy Crane
Garbs, Lisa Brown, Bonnie Likover, Shelley Haden,
Francie Willis, Mary Ann Belin, and Kim Watson. As the
word gets out, more and more women are joining forces

to rally their friends. Linda Dewhurst said, "It's not a matter of whether I can fit this in. It's so clear that this is where God is working. When we see God working, we have no choice but to join Him."

IN THE MIDST OF VICTORY, THERE IS ALWAYS A PRICE TO PAY

IN THE MOVIE "LUTHUR", MARTIN LUTHUR MADE THIS statement to his spiritual father, "When you sent me into the world to make a change, did you not think it would cost something?" Although God moved miraculously at supersonic speed, the beginning months after the separation of Inspire Women from the College of Biblical Studies felt like I was between a funeral and a new birth. I had to let go of the dreams I had for the College and at the College before I could fully receive God's new dream for my life. In the beginning months, I found myself weaving in and out of sadness. A friend of mine said, "Give yourself time to grieve. What you are feeling is normal." She told me I would find myself conducting meetings but as soon as the people left, I would face the stark aloneness of my journey. I learned that you can be in a crowd but still feel utterly alone.

I literally had to force myself to keep working when all I wanted to do was to crawl into bed and to stay there forever. Why do new beginnings require saying goodbye to the past? Why do we need to let go before we can move forward? I learned that faith is trusting God for something not yet visible to the human eye. Although I celebrated God's provision, the fact still remained that every morning I walked into an office space void of all the students who used to be part of my world. In a way, I had lost all my kids. The silence was deafening. The fact that there was no activity on the floor I was on except what I personally generated was such a stark contrast to the hustle and bustle of the students coming in and out of my office in between classes. Could I look at the emptiness and believe God that one day the office would come alive again? All the while I was saying to God, "Tell me once again why this separation was necessary. Tell me once again I did not misunderstand your calling."

Today, I walk into the Inspire Women offices and I see my "spiritual kids" rushing about with excitement and purpose (see Reflection Journal, p.243-261 Staff). They take for granted the activity and noise level. They are one big happy family. Even though they know how far God has carried us, I don't think anyone but the birth mother can fully understand the intensity of labor pain.

There were so many times I wanted to pick up the phone to call my spiritual father. But I knew that for this season, God separated us because he was cutting the umbilical cord. Dr. Boyd was in my life for a short time to help me believe in the gift God had put in me. Dr. Boyd was a priceless gift from God to teach me by his example what it means to persevere. The best way to honor him for the time he invested in my life is to succeed and to finish the task God has given me. At times, my heart still wishes we could journey together but I know it's time for me to walk the rest of the way with my heavenly Father. Are you in a place where you need to cut the umbilical cord so you can experience the miraculous with God?

"YOU JUMP AND I'LL PRAY!"

TO HELP ME THROUGH THE SHOCK OF THE SEPARATION, God gave me an incredible Board who rallied around me. God raised up Carol Byrd as a board member and my prayer warrior. Although she was not physically well enough to be in the office every day, she kept in contact with me through the telephone. She covered me in prayer before I went into any meeting and I would call her immediately afterwards to give her a full report. I felt God had given her to me as a physical reminder of His presence. Just hearing her voice gave me the confidence that I was not alone. There were days when I would say to her, "I feel like I'm jumping out of a plane without a parachute." She replied, "You jump and I'll pray." She never let me give up. Whenever I was discouraged, she spent more hours on her knees petitioning God's protection and favor.

Cathy Wining Thomas, another board member, was the top female executive at Conoco Phillips. She is now retired but worked tirelessly to sell tables for our fundraiser luncheon even when her husband was in the hospital. She did not waiver in her commitment to God's purpose and trusted God to give her the strength to endure. Cathy felt it was her calling to walk beside me and to help carry my burden in any way.

Theola Booker would break out in praise and song during our meetings. It was as if God filled her heart with His music which she then poured out to encourage us. Mia Wright was filled with the wisdom of the Holy Spirit and generously offered her counsel and her visionary leadership. It was Mia who came up with the idea to invite local leaders of different ethnicities to share their teaching platform. I always felt that Mia could run circles around me in her gift but she encouraged my leadership and encouraged me to trust God for the impossible. Marge Caldwell was in her nineties, but oh what insight she had for the ministry. There were times when we had to make hard decisions. We would kid Marge and say, "Marge, I thought you were a push over. We never realized you were this tough!" She would laugh and say, "Oh you decide, Anita, but this is what I think." I learned that when Marge thought something, I should go with it because she was always right.

One of my greatest blessings on the Inspire Women's board was my husband, Robert Carman. In the daytime, he worked in systems planning for Exxon Mobil. In the evenings and weekends, he worked tirelessly to create the infrastructure for Inspire Women. In spite of the thousands of transactions through the conference and the luncheon and our speaking engagements, Robert could tell me immediately where the organization was financially.

He guided me but he was careful not to take over even though I knew he could manage Inspire Women with his eyes closed. He encouraged and affirmed. The coaching he gave me reminded me of a little sister pedaling a bike with a big brother running behind her shouting, "You can do it! You can do it!" The greatest encouragement to me was his continuous assessment of where Inspire Women was yesterday compared to today and how amazed he was in how fast God was growing the organization. He said, "Inspire Women is blessing more and more women. What else could you want?"

I WAS IMPRESSED WITH WHAT GOD HAD DONE BUT HE WANTED TO DO MORE

BY NOVEMBER OF 2003, INSPIRE WOMEN REACHED nearly 4,000 women in one weekend event through a luncheon and conference. As soon as we had money in the bank and I felt some relief, God said, "Give it away." From the conference and other Inspire Women platforms, women were offered the opportunity to be trained to step into their calling. Though we started with zero in the bank in May of 2003, by December of 2003, Inspire Women established the Inspire Women scholarship fund in the amount of $100,000.

We could have kept the money in our own account and awarded the funds over the year to the scholarships recipients but I knew that December was always a hard financial challenge for the College of Biblical Studies. So, I scheduled a lunch with Dr. Boyd. During lunch, I handed Dr. Boyd the letter stating what the Inspire Women's Board had voted to give the College as a gift. We would pre-deposit $100,000 with the College so they could use the funds but we would choose the women who would be receiving the scholarships as God reveals to us those gems in the city He wants to send to the College. Tears started to roll down Dr. Boyd's face. He said, "Never in a million years would I have imagined another non-profit handing me a check for this amount. This is the kind of check that a business that makes millions of dollars writes, but not one non-profit to another."

By the Spring of 2004, Inspire Women established a scholarship fund to help students we would send for graduate studies at Dallas Theological Seminary. Since Inspire Women was an independent organization, we no longer existed just for the College of Biblical Studies. We were truly free to listen to God's dreams in women for ministry and to help them to be trained in the best programs in town that fit their calling. In a year and a half from the organization's humble beginnings in May of 2003, Inspire Women has invested over half a million dollars to inspire and to train women to step into God's purpose for their lives.

Is THERE A WRONG WAY TO
BEG FOR YOUR CHILDREN?

APPROXIMATELY SIXTY PERCENT OF THE WOMEN who request scholarship funding from Inspire Women come from backgrounds of abuse. In them, I see the story of Teresa and the little girl in the alley. What if they were to walk into my office today as an adult? If God had touched their lives and they came in to me and said, "I want to build off my pain to be a positive blessing to those who come from hurts similar to what I have experienced. Will you please train me to share the power of God's Word to help others find healing?" Oh, how my heart would go out to them. Oh, how I never would want them to go away with the message that God's people did not think they were worth their investment.

Forty percent of the women who request scholarship funding from Inspire Women are community or ministry leaders whose churches and families do not have the budget to train them for more effective ministry. I listen to the timid cry of a ministry leader who asks for help. She is not used to asking for anything for herself. She has always been the last on the totem pole. She is the kind of leader who, when confronted with a need, would offer to help someone else rather than taking the money to help herself. When discretionary income is low, her dreams are the last to be funded. Three specific incidents are etched in my heart.

In one case, the woman was the wife of a Pastor with a growing church. She said to me, "I don't feel adequate to help my husband as God gives us this growing church. I want to serve beside him but I feel he is moving way past where I am. Will you train me so I can be a better wife and helper?' I could even hear in her voice the words, "I don't feel I'm the right wife. I'm not smart enough. I can't keep up. Won't you help me so I can serve along side my husband?"

In a second case, the woman was a refugee from the Sudan. She was the choir director over 85 Sudanese women and wanted to learn how to teach them God's Word. Her desire was to one day return to her country and to bring God's Word back to her people.

In a third case, the woman was in her twenties. Her pastor found her homeless under a bridge. He and his wife took her into their home. She was growing strong spiritually and the Pastor wanted to train her to help oversee the women's ministry at his church. When Inspire Women offered to train her, the Pastor said, "No one has ever offered to help me train up women who could help me in the work at my church." His church reaches out to those from backgrounds of addiction.

As I appeal on behalf of the women, I beg the Lord to give me the wisdom to communicate clearly. I do not have any training in fund raising. I violate so many unspoken rules without intending to offend. I said to the Lord, "I don't understand why you have put this burden on my heart. There are people who are trained to raise money. I go as a mother who is asking for a bowl of spiritual rice for her children. I don't know how to ask the right way. Is there a wrong way to beg for your children?" When I accidentally step on someone's toes, I beg the Lord for forgiveness. Oh, heaven forbid that my inadequacies would hurt one of my sisters.

God reminds me that my work takes me into many subcultures. There is no formula or science and sometimes the only way to learn the rules in a subculture is to make mistakes. At the end of the day, I find myself saying "I'm sorry" over and over again. At the end of the day, I must trust that as long as I am driven with a passion to connect with God's heart, then His grace will cover me. I pray that those I appeal to will see that I am but a mother who is appealing for her children. At the end of the day, perhaps they will see that there is no wrong way to beg for your children.

A SPIRITUAL FORCE TO BE RECKONED WITH

THE FULL POWER OF GOD'S KINGDOM WILL BE released when we empower all God's daughters to represent Him in the world. When I look over the scholarship applications and see a young single woman who spent two years learning Mandarin in China just so she can bring the gospel to that nation, I see God raising up women to change the world. I ask myself, "Are we sending our spiritual warriors into battle with the proper ammunition?" This applicant was asking Inspire Women to train her in a biblical program in cross cultural outreach for the purpose of returning full time to evangelize the Chinese in China. The women who are coming to Inspire Women are compelled by their heavenly Father's voice to represent Him in the world. They are taking His healing words into the prisons, abuse centers, veterans hospitals, crisis pregnancy centers, and numerous ministries in their city and throughout the world.

To my cry from years ago, "God, why don't you do something?" is God's answer, "I have done something. I raised up Inspire Women to help women connect their lives with my purpose." Not only for women from abuse backgrounds but for so many women who never had an advocate to guard God's dream for their lives, God moves to protect His daughters and to release the full potential for His work on earth.

Recently, I was a guest at an event to honor our military. One of the sergeants said, "When I wear this uniform, I disappear. All you see is the uniform of the United States Army and you see the flag on my sleeves that represent the United States of America." Then he added, "I want you to know that we are a force to be reckoned with."

As I left that event, God impressed these words on my heart, "I have daughters who have barely survived backgrounds of abuse and abandonment who are asking to return to the battle field so they can rescue those with suffering similar to what they have endured. I have other daughters who are willing to lay down their lives in service for the souls of those in their own city and throughout the world. They will go into the hardest battles and travel to the remotest parts of the world in my name. They are not asking for training to gain anything for themselves. They carry my banner over them and they are a spiritual force to be reckoned with." When I enter the sanctuary of my prayer time with God, I hear Him say, "Go boldly to rally your city to ensure the perpetual existence of Inspire Women as a friend to my daughters. Invite my people to sow into an endowment to ensure that when a woman desires to be trained for my service, you will not turn anyone away. Do not send them into battle without the proper ammunition. Create a trust fund for their training in my name as my irrefutable message to my daughters that I have heard their cries, I am taking steps to protect their potential, I love them with all my heart, and I trust them with my mission."

ONCE HE SPEAKS, I AM HELD ACCOUNTABLE FOR WHETHER I OBEY

ONE MORNING I REMEMBER COMING DOWN THE stairs totally fatigued. I said to my oldest son, "Robbie, my life is not normal. No one lives this way." He said, "Mommy, eagles fly alone." I said, "I don't want to be an eagle. I want to be a chicken and cluck around like the rest." He said, "The problem is, you don't get to choose, God is the one who has chosen." I said to him, "Son, there's something very wrong with you. That is not a normal answer for a teenager!"

My younger son, Thomas said, "Mom, you can't give up because Inspire Women helps a lot of people." Thomas has not changed much since he was eight. I remember quite some years ago, I was invited to go to Bolivia to encourage the missionaries who wanted to give up and return to America. At the time, there were riots going on in the city. There was fear that a Christian gathering might be considered illegal and I might get arrested for speaking at a conference. I brought this concern before my family. I said to my kids, "What if Mommy doesn't come back? What if I'm arrested and am stuck in jail?" Thomas said, "Mommy, you have to go. If you don't go, the missionaries might get discouraged and leave. Then thousands will die without knowing Jesus." Then he added. "I don't want their blood to be on my conscience!" In the words of my children, I have found hope for the future. Could it be that instead of beating our heads on a rock to rescue dreams that God allowed to die, we are to re-channel the energy towards a dream that will help those who still have a chance to live? Instead of focusing on dreams that won't die, could it be that what God wants our hearts to remember are the dreams His heart longs for?

I used to think, "If God would only tell me what He wanted from me, I would do it." So I blamed God for my lack of focus. The truth was, God was silent because He knew I wasn't about to do what He cared about. I would waste time arguing or telling God why my idea was better. So, in His grace, He waited for me to be ready before He spoke His marching orders. It never occurred to me that once He speaks, I am held accountable for whether I obey. Compelled by His love, God remains silent and waits until we understand that we do not choose our assignments. Then He speaks and our response determines how our names will go down in spiritual history.

When Jill Briscoe, an internationally known Bible teacher and author reported her ministry highlights around the world, I saw God raising up replicas of Jill through Inspire Women in response to the spiritual hunger in the world. Jill agreed to help shape the training of leaders like herself at Inspire Women packaged with other classes through programs in the city that best fit a woman's calling. One day, the leadership internship program offered through Inspire Women will serve as certification of demonstrated servant leadership, a commanding knowledge of God's Word, and a willingness to bring the gospel into their communities and to the ends of the earth.

Below was Jill's newsletter. Can you imagine the potential that will be released for God's kingdom when we inspire women across ethnicities and denominations to be agents for Jesus who God can send to represent Him powerfully?

BRISCOE BULLETIN: JILL IN PRISON
WEDNESDAY, FEBRUARY 23, 2005
(REPRINTED BY PERMISSION WWW.TELLINGHTETURTH.ORG)

"I WAS IN PRISON AND YOU VISITED ME NOT..."

Last month Stuart and I were in Russia, training Christian leaders from the Caucuses where some of the churches they are planting are the first in the country. I knew these leaders were going back to places Christ had not yet been named, where to profess Him was dangerous and only a handful of believers had come to faith.

As Stuart and I were teaching, the men and women in front of us listened with great attention. I was teaching the book of Philippians. We marveled together how anyone could write the words: "Rejoice in the Lord always - I will say it again rejoice. Be anxious for nothing...and the peace of God will garrison your heart." And then, "I have learned in whatsoever state I am to be content" - written FROM PRISON!

At the end of my teaching time the Russians asked me where I would be going in the next few months so they could pray for me. "Among other things, I'm going to prison in Texas," I said. "There are eleven thousand prisoners in the middle of this state, and a friend who works in chaplaincy has invited me to spend a week in three of those facilities teaching in chapel, going cell to cell, and encouraging the volunteers from churches who minister there."

Three couples came to me at the end of my talk and said, "We work in jails in Dagestan. Some of us, like the prisoners in Gatesville, have been incarcerated not for Christ but for crimes, but we found the Lord in jail. Others of us have been imprisoned for our faith. Now we have a ministry to the men and women in the jails we were in. We want to send a letter to our sisters and brothers in Gatesville, Texas. Will you take it?" I put the precious letter carefully in my Bible.

When I got to prison in Texas, I felt a little disorientated. Paul was in prison suffering for Christ's sake, while those I mingled with in Texas were suffering prison as a result of crimes committed. Not one was there because they were a Christian. Could I bring the same message to these inmates from Paul, in chains for Christ from the book of Philippians, that I had been teaching to church planters in Russia? I decided I could.

What do Dagestan, Russia and Gatesville, Texas have in common? Prisons! Prisons with people in them - lots of people. There are differences of course. In Dagestan, the women who give birth to babies while in jail keep them with them in their cells for three years and then the government takes them away. Few see them again. In one prison there are over three hundred children, I was told.

In Gatesville, Texas, where eleven thousand prisoners are housed, there are no children in the cells with their mothers. But I soon learned the men and women have much in common with the mothers and fathers in Dagestan jails. They desperately miss their kids. The heart hunger is acute. The pain and emotion make it difficult to breathe as they tell you about their children. Oh, the tears!

I read the letter from the Russian believers to each chapel full of prisoners. In some of the chapels we could not talk to the women, who were not allowed to stand or sing. In others groups, we could stand at the door as they left and get our arms around them and hug them close, breathing a prayer over each as they lined up to return to their cells.

Many sat still as statues and heard the words of grace and love: words of Paul from prison from the book of Philippians, and the love and promises of prayers from people in Russia half a world away. People who had found there is no sin too big for God to forgive. It was as if we had walked into a terminal cancer ward and offered a cure!

I learned that many in this place had come to faith. "It's easy here," the Christian workers told me. "We don't need to convince anyone in Gatesville jail that they're sinners!" I pondered the thought that it was harder to deal with "good sinners" who go to church, than "bad sinners who turn to crime" who don't!

"How good do you have to be to go to heaven?" asked an inmate.

"Perfect," I replied.

"Then who can go?"

"Only those imperfect people - which is the whole human race - who have been forgiven their imperfection."

"And how do you get a pardon like that?" How indeed!

What joy to tell them the story of Barabbas and how he was a sinner caught, tried, condemned, and sentenced to death for murder and insurrection. I painted the picture of the guards coming and opening his cell door and telling him he was a free man. (I saw the wondering comprehension in the eyes in front of me!) As Barabbas was caught up in the mob on the way to Calvary, he followed and found his cross there, fully occupied.

I imagined out loud what might have happened. I pictured Barabbas asking John, who seemed to know the man on his cross, who the stranger was. Just who had taken his place? John explained that this was a man called Jesus. He who had healed lepers, opened the eyes of the blind, and loved the world that hated Him had said He was the Savior of the world, come to save mankind from the eternal consequences of their sin by being their substitute. Barabbas, I told them, looked at Jesus on the middle cross and simply said, "He's there instead of me! He's taking my place and punishment!"

Some of the women listening intently "got it" and prayed with me. Others cursed the volunteers out, decided to take their chances with a Holy God, and chose to drown in their hatred and hardness of heart. It's a choice you know!

Chapel after chapel I had the privilege of standing before hundreds of women in prison garb, in the maximum block with death row cells in plain view, or in the reception facility with wide, frightened-eyed newcomers being processed. (Some looking heartbreakingly as young as my seven teenage grandchildren.) These women had just been given their number. From now on this would be their identity.

I read the letter from the Russian believers and talked

about Paul and the peace of God that passes understanding. I explained that the peace 'of' God is only possible when you have been reconciled and have peace 'with' God. They cried. I cried. God cried!

The women who were allowed to interact with us were moved mostly by three things. First, they had never heard about the persecuted church before. They could not believe that people would risk a life sentence in jail for being a Christian. To voluntarily risk jail or worse for Jesus because He went to death row and was executed for crimes He didn't commit - their crimes - blew them away!

The second thing they wanted to talk about was the children in prison. To think of having babies in prison and keeping them with them for three years, and then to have them taken away overwhelmed them. Tears flowed again as I read from the Russian letter: "We are trying to have a home for these children in the Russian prison till the mother is released so there may be reconciliation. It's hard going though, and much opposition. Please pray for us."

The third thing that made a deep impact was a story I told about meetings I had taken a few years back in a country where Christians were being persecuted. Thirty-six women huddled in an attic for five days of the first Bible teaching they had ever received. Bibles were not allowed in that land. They had made their way to the upper room willing to turn up at the possible cost of their freedom or even life itself. We taught from eight in the morning to six at night for five days straight. And this without notes! They begged us to teach after supper too!

The third day I asked them, "Do you want to worship? I would love to hear you sing one of your hymns." There were excited murmurs among them and my sweet young interpreter said, "Oh, that would be wonderful."

I waited. They sang and the hair went up on the back of my neck. They sang in a whisper! My partner and I listened, greatly moved, and I vowed I would never sing loudly and lustily in church again without praying for my sisters in that attic, who could only whisper in case they would be discovered. At that point, I had absolutely NO idea why I was led to share that story with the inmates of Gatesville prison.

The next day some volunteers ate with the inmates. Silence was the rule. This was a surprise as we didn't know the women were forbidden to talk in many of these venues. Some inmates were on duty in the kitchen. Our team members took their plates and walked to the kitchen hatch with them, under the watchful eyes of the strict guards. They caught their breath, as from the inmates who were washing up came the whisper of a familiar melody, "This little light of mine, I'm going to let it shine..." The women forbidden to talk were singing in a whisper! It was a whisper of grace barely heard. Their eyes watchful widened as the guard suddenly appeared and caught the barely heard worship. The women stopped, nervous and fearful of the guard, and the atmosphere became electric. The guard paused and then, unbelievably, joined in like tones, "Let it shine, let it shine, let it shine!" Unheard of! The Jesus lovers in the kitchen took up the whispered words as they, given permission, completed their song and task.

In a few months, I will be returning to that attic room in a country half way round the globe, and you can be sure I will take with me the thanks of some sisters, new in Christ in Gatesville prison, who, thanks to them, have found a way to worship hitherto forbidden!

Sitting quietly in a room in California, as I write this, I pause - to cry again. I had run to the deep place where nobody goes and sat on the steps of my soul. Then I heard His voice as He came close and sat with me. I looked at Him. There was something I didn't quite understand, something to do with his clothes.

"Thank you for visiting me, Jill!"

"I am ashamed, Lord. It's only taken me how many years? Help me make up for lost time!" There was quietude then, and I thought about the faces in Gatesville.

"I miss them all already, Lord, especially the sixteen year old who looks so like our granddaughter, and that frightened little squirrel who doesn't know what to do with herself for the next seventeen years."

I was in prison and you visited me," He said quietly. "Come again."

Then I realized why He looked different. He had on prison clothes.

GOD HOLDS OUR HEARTACHE IN HIS HANDS

WHEN DREAMS WON'T DIE, REMEMBER THAT NEW beginnings begin with you. At some point, you cannot live off the fumes of a dream from yesteryears. Is it time for you to step out into God's new story for your life? Is it time for you to allow God to choose His dream for you?

God is perfectly able to orchestrate events to walk you into His perfect plan. In the midst of my getting through life, God was weaving a tapestry. He wove a strand of golden thread through Christine Petcher, the missionary's daughter I met while a freshman...

...through Campus Crusade for Christ during my College days

...through Pastor Phil Meiss and his wife Mary when I was a single career woman

...through that little missionary church in Brussels Belgium

...through Alice Peacock my first leader in Bible Study Fellowship

…through Beth Moore's Sunday School class

…through Dallas Theological Seminary

…through Dr. Boyd, the President of the College of Biblical Studies

…till He cut the umbilical cord and led me out Himself to establish Inspire Women.

Before I was born He knew me and He had already marked my moments in His story. Although life may not make sense, although events seem random, will you look for God's fingerprints in the midst of the confusion? Will you do the next right thing? Will you walk through the best open door that aligns with God's character and purpose? Will you allow God to entrust you with a dream His heart longs for?

There will be moments in your journey when you will need to make a choice. I had to decide, "Do I accept Beth Moore's invitation to teach? Do I accept the College's invitation to plan a citywide women's conference? Do I walk away from my spiritual father and trust God to take me into His future?" Are you at a point in your life where you must choose to step out in faith and allow God to write a new story for your life?

I used to ask God what's taking Him so long and why can't He hurry? Today I find myself asking Him to slow down. The Lord said, "All this time, you told me to hurry!" That was the last time I ever told God what to do. Today I say, "Just take your time, Lord. I don't need anything to happen. I would be perfectly happy if life was just you and me!" But God won't allow life to be some artificial world of just you and Him because He is on a mission. He is working with a world that is scheduled to end. He knows He only has so much time before the curtain will fall and the cosmic play on planet earth will be over. On that day, what happens to us in eternity will be determined by our choices in this world. He is trying to get millions to make the right choices before it's too late.

When your heart is holding on to dreams that won't die know that God sees the tears. King David said in Psalm 56:8, "Record my lament; list my tears on your scroll — are they not in your record?" Realize that when God holds our heartache in His hands, it is only a matter of time before God goes into action. His mercy is what compels Him. Oh how exciting to know that God is about to do a new thing. However, recognize that God has dreams of His own and we were created for His purpose. I pray you will hear your Father's voice as He says to you, "Arise daughter of a King and go boldly to reflect my image and heart to the world. For this was why I created you. Do not let your past imprison you or limit you. Your past is not an excuse for a lesser ministry but my opportunity for a greater one. Do not stay in the paralysis of facts you cannot change. Instead, receive the message that all things were created for me and by me. Do not let fear paralyze you. Perfect love casts out all fear. Go with the boldness in my name. When I am with you, no human can thwart my plans."

Oh Faithful One, are you ready to receive the fresh winds from heaven and to live a life filled with passion and energy? You will discover the reason for which you were created when you lose your story to give God what He longs for.

5

What's It All For?

When all hope for the fulfillment of a dream is gone but the dream refuses to die, what do you do with that groaning within your heart? -- This autobiography and reflection journal was born from the heart of a disciple who pounded on heaven's door with this very question.

In the personal reflection journal that accompanies this autobiography, I have shared the Word of God that set me free. It is my prayer that you, too, will be set free. God has been my wise counselor. He alone has entangled the knots in my past. He can be your counselor as well.

When I began writing, I had two dreams that I laid on the altar: One was the broken dream of my mother who took her own life and never made it to the Promise Land of America. God took care of my feelings of abandonment by hand raising me for Himself. From heaven's throne, He heard the cry from a young girl's heart and out of grace alone, He lowered His hand and lifted me from the miry pit. He took my lack of identity and He gave me a royal heritage. He breathed His life into my being and sealed me with His Holy Spirit. He claimed me as His own and made me a child of God, the daughter of a King. He took my lack of security and He planted the rock of all ages beneath my feet. He took my lack of purpose and gave me His royal commission. I would be an ambassador for Christ, a messenger of His hope to all the world.

My dream of reaching America with my mother by my side was transformed and resurrected with His eternal breath. May I share with you how God wrote the final chapter to my family's tragedy? Is there a chapter in your life that you need to pen the words "The End"? If so, I pray you will ask God to show you how to end the chapter.

You see, He is the author and finisher of our faith (Hebrews 12:2). He who began a good work in us will complete it (Philippians 1:6). No matter how badly we have distorted the script, when we return the pen to our Maker's hand, He is able to write a glorious ending. Below was a page from my personal journal.

> *The year is 1996. I am alone in my living room in the free land of America. In my hands, I hold a carry-on travel bag. The bag is ordinary looking and misleading. I unzip the bag, and I see a brown padded package from the Hong Kong Funeral Home. I cut the string, tear open the rough paper and my fingers feel the coolness of a smooth white glistening marble urn. On it are the gold etched letters of my mother's name and the words, "Rest in Peace".*
>
> *I had anticipated this moment so many times and had delayed it for fear of my own emotions. Would my promise to bring her to the Promise Land of America be fulfilled in this way? But, to my surprise, my heart is filled with a song because of what God has done to transform my suffering. "For God so loved the world, that He gave His only begotten Son, that whoever believes in Him should not perish, but have eternal life (John 3:16). In those words of the Bible, an exchange had taken*

place. On that cross, God crucified with His Son all the sins of the world, all the unfairness, all the injustices, all the broken dreams. God took it all and in return, He offered us the resurrection and the power for new beginnings. I knew then that the choice was mine. I could remain in the tragedy of my family's story or I could choose to proclaim a greater story. I could live my life in bondage to the past, or I could allow God to crucify my past to the cross and be set free into new life. The power was available, and I chose to receive it.

I know my mother is not in this urn. She is in the arms of God, and I can think of no other place that is safer. After all these years, I still don't have all my answers but I don't need them either. As I look at this urn, I praise God for the fulfillment of a promise. This urn closes a chapter to my life. This urn tells of the heart of a daughter who has not forgotten, because "Mom, I love you. I will always love you, and I got you out before June 30, 1997, just as I promised. And Mom, your children are doing fine because our God is faithful. He remembered your prayers, and He hid your children under His wings. He repaired our dream and gave us a new tomorrow."

God is the ultimate dream repairer. He will transform the broken pieces of yesterday into a royal vessel fit for a King. Don't ever underestimate God. He hears our prayers, He remembers every tear. The story isn't over yet. And in the end, God wins. So will we. May we always remember that He created us for victory.

The other dream I had to lay down on the altar was quite unexpected. In my excitement to pick up the resurrected life God had given me, I was completely consumed with setting the world on fire for God. I didn't realize for my passions to soar for His glory, they had to be reigned in, put under His yoke, and purified.

I had not realized I wanted the blessing more than the suffering. I looked in the mirror and saw I was a coward at heart, a fool who had forgotten that glory has a price. In my desire for significance, I had forgotten that "...unless a kernel of wheat falls to the ground and dies, it remains only a single seed. But if it dies, it produces many seeds (John 12:24)." I had forgotten, "Unless I am willing to die for my Christ, I am not ready to live for Christ."

Like Peter who responded to Jesus' probing question, "Do you love me?" I found myself saying, "Lord, you know all things ...." I was embarrassed, ashamed, humbled. But, just as Jesus picked Peter up, I felt the arms of my Lord around me, picking me up and leading me forward.

I began to celebrate my "non-appointments". God's truth in Acts 17:26-27 resonated within me.

> **Acts 17:26-27** From one man he made every nation of men, that they should inhabit the whole earth; and he determined the times set for them and the exact places where they should live. God did this so that men would seek him and perhaps reach out for him and find him, though he is not far from each one of us.

Oh, how could I have missed such a treasure? God planted me in my time and space, God ordained every appointment and "non-appointment" for the ultimate purpose that I may find Him.

Was this what the Apostle Paul meant when He said in Philippians 3:14, "I press on toward the goal to win the prize for which God has called me heavenward in Christ Jesus..."? How did I miss that the prize is "in Christ Jesus"? Could it be that the prize that we so often set our eyes on is not the prize at all? I thought I could have more of life by having a bigger piece of an opportunity, an accomplishment or an earthly relationship. My Father's ultimate design is for me to have more of life by having more of Himself.

In Matthew 5:8, Jesus said, "Blessed are the pure in heart, for they will see God." When I offer my life totally and purely, I already have my reward. Have you ever thought about the awesomeness of actually seeing God? Be honest. What is your greatest treasure? Would you trade it to get a glimpse of God?

I used to think in terms of all the things I wanted to do for God. I had set myself up for discontent, with one more goal always dangling before me. God taught me to receive Jesus as my goal. He fills me to overflowing and it is out of my abundance that I will walk this earth with His authority and reach lives with His heart.

Having Jesus as my goal is to live in celebration of my relationship and allowing the results of my activity to fall where they will. Goals are wonderful for accountability and direction but when our destination is a "thing" rather than a person, we are left with a big void in our hearts.

Never in a million years did I expect God to entrust me with a ministry like Inspire Women. It was only when my dream was to sail with Jesus into the sunset that He could trust me with His dreams. I find myself wanting what He wants. I no longer ask, "Is this what I care about?" Instead, I find myself saying, "A calling is when God trusts you with something His heart longs for."

If you visited the Inspire Women's offices, one of the

sayings you will hear the staff say is this, "The best part of the journey is YOU!" We are in donated office space and move to another part of the building when the space is leased out. We believe that even in this exercise, God reminds us of our priorities. He alone is all that we need. When we work where He is working, we are in the safest place on planet earth. The best part of the journey is also all the friends God draws into Inspire Women to be part of His miracle. Our ultimate dream is to reach the mountaintop together. Oh how incredible it would be for Houston to be the first to raise an endowment to ensure biblical training for all God's daughters for generations to come. Oh the privilege to finish such a legacy together!

As we end our time together, I pray we have placed our hands a little tighter in the hands of Jesus. The harvest is plentiful and there is much work left to be done. As long as we are on this side of eternity, I pray that we will move with the momentum of our heavenly Father. Jesus said in John 5:17, "My Father is always at his work to this very day, and I, too, am working." The sheep are scattered and God is summoning us to go forward as a child of God, the son or daughter of a King, hand-picked by His grace, anointed with His power, compelled by His voice to reclaim this world for His kingdom.

Oh Faithful One, my precious co-laborer in Christ, what will you do with the rest of your life? What dreams will you live for? Oh, how I pray that we will join forces and help all women to connect with God's purpose and pour our lives into the dreams God's heart longs for. May we march across this land with His authority, exercising our calling to represent His mission. May we engage our passions and exercise our giftedness for His purpose. May we labor and persevere to join God in what He is doing and for the only prize that matters - that of seeing Jesus face to face.

When I pray for you, I hear a victory song. I believe in you because I believe in the power of God's Word in you as you put His Word into action.

Love,

Anita Grace Lie Carman

Epilogue

IN AN UNPRECEDENTED MOVE FOR A DONOR TOWARDS a grassroots women's organization, Inspire Women received a pledge to ensure the perpetual existence of the organization as a gift to the women of the city. In January of 2005, a donor committed to the monthly support to cover basic expenses of the organization with provision through estate planning for a perpetual gift of the same level.

The Inspire women's luncheon is projected to generate $250,000 a year towards program costs and scholarships. To close the gap between the projected need and what the luncheon generates, Inspire Women is raising an endowment in the amount of $7.5 million dollars.

How will the story end? In his farewell speech to the elders in the church at Ephesus, the Apostle Paul said in Acts 20:20-21, "You know that I have not hesitated to preach anything that would be helpful to you but have taught you publicly and from house to house. I have declared to both Jews and Greeks that they must turn to God in repentance and have faith in our Lord Jesus." Anita Carman says, "How will the story end for me and the staff personally? Similar to the Apostle Paul's momentum, my prayer is that the staff and I will say with a clear conscience that we stayed the course and did not hesitate to build the dream God entrusted to us. We have already received our prize because Jesus is our prize as we have labored where He is working. Now it's the turn of God's saints. How will their story end? Will they leave a life statement that they did not hesitate? Will they discern God's hand in their community and step into their moment in the history God is writing?"

TESTIMONIES: "Lord, what do you want from me?"

A SINGLE PROFESSIONAL'S
MONTHLY GIFT

MY NAME IS **JUDY HORNE**. I AM A SINGLE PROFESSIONAL with 24 years in the corporate world. I waited with great anticipation to attend "Living in the Miraculous", the class Anita Carman began teaching in January 2005. As I looked around the room, the audience was diverse, much like you would expect at a meeting of the United Nations. I felt the unmistakable presence of almighty God as Anita taught His word and shared the amazing story of how God raised up Inspire Women to equip women to fulfill God's calling on their lives.

Week after week it was though I could hear and feel God's heart beat as He opened my spiritual eyes to show me this ministry was unique and something His heart longed for. A tremendous tug of war ensued within

because it never occurred to me there were women who
desired to serve God in ministry who did not have the
finances to obtain training. These women were not asking
to be trained to get a job. They were asking for help to
better reach abused children, people in the homeless shel-
ters, prison inmates, the lost souls in third world countries. They were reaching those I could not reach. The
least I could do was to send them into battle with adequate
spiritual ammunition.

Over the next four weeks the Lord put an unquench-
able desire in my heart to somehow be a part of what He
was doing through Inspire so I began to prayerfully seek
His will. God led me to make a one-time donation but
deep within I knew He wanted more. With a restless spirit void of peace I continued to ask, "Lord, what do you
want from me?". I made the commitment to do whatever
God led me to do. My Heavenly Father wanted me to support Inspire on a monthly basis but I did not see how that
was possible given my current financial obligations. But
God showed me how to reorganize my finances and make
some minor changes to my discretionary spending to support Inspire. Immediately, I felt God's overwhelming
peace return as I stepped out in faith. Since my monthly
commitment, I was blessed with a bonus from work. After
tithing my bonus, I donated the entire amount to Inspire.

I have always believed that you cannot out-give God.
His word tells us "To whom much is given, much is
required" and "He that is faithful with little is given
much". Everything I have belongs to God and He blesses

us to be a blessing to others. I met some of the scholarship applicants and recipients. These were truly "woman after God's own heart". You cannot be in the same room without feeling their passion to serve others selflessly for God's glory. I realized God's divine plan has a specific role for each of us. Mine is to share what God has so richly and faithfully blessed me with to enable His work to be done on earth. There is no greater excitement than to know you have been a part of equipping others before sending them into the battles of life.

A DAUGHTER'S INHERITANCE
AND ESTATE GIFT

CAROL BYRD HAS A HEART DISEASE, AND DURING A TIME when she was bedridden, she cried out to God for an opportunity to make a difference for Him. God wove Carol's life into Anita Carman's. As God put the ministry of Inspire Women on Anita's platter, Carol was on her knees for hours every day petitioning God to open doors and provide for the ministry.

When Inspire Women started with zero in the bank, Anita told Carol, "We are jumping out the plane without a parachute." Carol replied, "You jump and I'll pray." As Inspire Women moved into over 2,000 square feet of donated office space, Carol praised, "God is so good. That's what I had prayed for." Even as she was bed-ridden by her own ailing heart, Carol never missed one heartbeat of Inspire Women. It was as if God used Carol's heart to give Inspire Women a strong heartbeat.

One day, in her prayer time, Carol told the Lord she wanted to give Him a cherished possession. So, Carol left a ranch she had inherited from her father to the Inspire Women Endowment Fund in her estate planning. She asked God what He wanted for His land and listed it on the market accordingly. Carol is praying that her gift will inspire others to give sacrificially to ensure all God's daughters the privilege of being trained in God's Word. Carol affirms, "I pray with confidence knowing that God trusts His daughters to share His message of hope."

A VOLUNTEER'S OBSERVATIONS
OF THE INSIDE STORY

MY NAME IS GRETCHEN BROWNING. I became involved with Inspire Women through a fundraiser luncheon that a friend invited me to attend. I remember thinking at the luncheon that I should start supporting this organization financially. What fun that would be "writing checks, receiving thanks and accolades from people for being such a nice person. I would be "doing"something "for" God. Yes, as a new Christian I was still being driven by worldly ideas and thinking. But God had other plans.

Shortly after attending that luncheon, my world turned upside down and was shaken with a godly force. I found myself in an entirely different financial position. My resources were dwindling and I soon found myself with an extra amount of time on my hands.

Talking life over with God one day, I asked what He wanted me to do with this extra time. Where did He want my hands doing His work? At that time, communication from God was slightly out of tune for me, so I promised that if He would only be clear and direct, I would be obedient and respond immediately to His direction. God placed Inspire Women before me and said, "Get to work".

I called Inspire Women to see what kind of help they needed and even though Anita was out of town, she called me back immediately and said, "Of course we need help, how many hours a week should we count on?" This was my first personal interaction with Anita Carman and I learned a big lesson about Anita: "Always say Yes" to God's prompting and then trust Him to show you how later.

While volunteering at Inspire Women I heard the staff talking, I listened to their testimonies and I soon realized that they were trying to raise their own salary support while working a minimum of 9 to 11 hours a day without benefits. I thought, "Why would anyone do that?" I truly wondered what kind of strange people I had gotten involved with? There was no way that I would ever put myself in that kind of position. Then, God began doing His thing.

Though my world had changed, each week that I volunteered at Inspire Women I saw a new example of God's almighty hand.Women's hearts and lives were being touched and made whole by God and His Word. With my

own eyes I saw unexpected donations being given anony-
mously to support Inspire Women's ministry. All this cannot be attributed to a human being, but only to God.

At times it was frustrating to me to see how frugal the
organization operated in expenses that would make their
lives so much easier. However, I began to understand how
dedicated the organization was in appealing for services
to be donated so they could invest their funds in the
women of the city. Anita made expense decisions based
on what was best for the training of women that God had
entrusted to her. The more I learned, the more amazed I
became. It was so refreshing to see God's hand working
so visibly.

Miracles just seem to happen at Inspire Women.
When a need arises, God opens a door for the need to be
met. Like the day I was with several friends and made a
joking comment about the need to bring the organization's
data handling into the 21st century. One of my friends
said, "If you are serious I want to help. I love doing that
very kind of programming and that is what I've been
doing for the last several years at work." So, we have
started the process and are very excited about what this
will mean to the Inspire Women's staff. It will make their
work time much more efficient.

I thought I was there to bless Inspire Women's staff
and the scholarship recipients. Again, God had another
plan. God's very visible almighty working hand at Inspire
Women has comforted me, ministered to me, and given
me renewed hope. I'll never forget the day when Joan, one

of the staff, said, "What is going on? Let's talk." Or the day Anita said, "What do you think of this? Let's talk." I was an accepted part of the team where God was working so visibly. I was thrilled!

Only God could have worked all this together to support His daughters. I am thrilled to be working with God at Inspire Women. Won't you come join us?

Inspire! WOMEN'S *Friendship Circle*

INVESTING IN WOMEN WHO CHANGE THE WORLD

Anita,

How exciting to know that Inspire Women is providing ongoing help and raising an endowment to ensure the funds for women for biblical training for generations to come. I am delighted to join you in leaving a legacy to bless God's daughters across ethnicities and denominations.

I understand Inspire Women's events cast a wide net to search for God's gems in our community. I praise God for the nearly 60% scholarship applicants who come from backgrounds of abuse who are returning to the battle grounds they barely survived, in order to reach those who are still suffering. I bless the 40% who are ministry leaders who are selfless in their service but whose churches and families do not have the budget to equip them with spiritual ammunition and tools for more effective ministry.

I am broken hearted to know of potential that is being lost to share God's Word unless we intervene. It is my privilege to invest in women who desire to change the world with God's Word. Please include me in the **Inspire Women's Friendship Circle**. Where my heart is, there is my treasure. Please receive the following gift from my heart to yours and to my heavenly Father.

Inspire! WOMEN'S Friendship Circle

INVESTING IN WOMEN WHO CHANGE THE WORLD

First Name: Dr./Mr./Mrs./Ms._____

Last Name:_____

Address: _____

City: _____ State: _____ Zip: _____ Email: _____

Hm Phone: _____ Cell: _____ Wk Ph: _____

Church Name:_____ Company Name: _____

·············· **WHAT IS GOD LEADING YOU TO GIVE?** ··············

☐ A monthly gift of $_____ (Please give whatever you can).

☐ A percentage of _____% from any bonus I receive this year or from a windfall from a business venture.

☐ $_____ or _____% from my inheritance. Please contact me for details.

☐ A one time amount of $_____.

Please apply my gift to the following (Check one of the following)

☐ Any need you have at Inspire Women

☐ Registrations to seminars/conferences and scholarships to programs that best fit a woman's calling.

(Programs Inspire Women has supported include College of Biblical Studies, Dallas Theological Seminary, South Western Seminary, Moody Bible Institute Distance Learning, Precepts Training Institute)

·············· **PAYMENT INFORMATION** ··············

☐ Enclosed is my check for $_____

☐ Please charge my credit card: Amex / Visa/ Master/ Discover

A monthly amount of $_____ until otherwise notified; a one time amount of $_____

Card #: _____ Expiration: _____

Name on card: _____ Your Signature:_____

Complete form and mail or fax to:
6524 San Felipe #516 • Houston, Texas 77057 • Tel: (713)521-1400 • Fax: (713)521-1388
If you wish to sow into the endowment fund, please call Anita at (713)521-1796

Appendix

Speakers and Community Leaders Who Encouraged **Inspire Women**

The Women Inspire Women Reaches

WHO DOES INSPIRE WOMEN REACH?	HOW DOES INSPIRE WOMEN REACH THEM?
Those who wish to start their week with God's Word and enjoy an e-discipleship relationship that offers researched answers from the Bible.	A weekly e-devotional that reaches the mailbox of the recipient every Monday morning. Ability to tap into an e-discipleship ministry and email questions about life. As of June of 2005, there are over 6,000 on the weekly email list.
Those God is drawing to connect their lives to His greater purpose.	Citywide conferences and events that casts a wide net into the city in search of God's gems "On the road" bible classes in different geographic locations in the city. Speaking engagements at women's luncheons and retreats in various organizations and churches.
Those who are ready to take the step into their God-given purpose.	For the many churches in our city that have limited resources to develop the potential in their women, Inspire Women offers: • Online assessment of a woman's unique gifts. • Leadership classes to help women surrender their dreams for God's dreams; to discern His voice; to take steps to put the dream into motion. • A leadership discipleship program and certificate for those Inspire Women selects for more personalized training to help women bring the teaching from the Inspire Women's Leadership Formation Center back to their home churches and to train leaders throughout the world.
Those who need specialized or more formal accredited training to prepare for their calling.	The Inspire Women's scholarship program funds scholarships for the certificate, undergraduate and graduate levels in programs that will best prepare a woman for her calling such as a Masters in Biblical Counseling; a certificate in how to teach the Bible. Distance learning is also provided for those who have young children at home or are in a season in life where they are home bound.

In the past year and a half, Inspire Women invested over $500,000 in the inspiration and the training of women for ministry. Women serve in abuse centers, prisons, veterans hospitals, youth centers, pregnancy crisis centers, women's ministry, missions, etc. Approximately 60% of scholarship applicants come from backgrounds of abuse and use their training to build from their past pain to positively minister to those from similar backgrounds. 40% are community and ministry leaders whose churches and families do not have the income to train them for more effective ministry outreach.

Speakers & Honorees
at the Inspire Women's Luncheon

Inspire Awards Fundraiser Luncheon				
2001	2002	2003	2004	2005
KEYNOTE SPEAKERS				
Ruth Graham McIntrye *Daughter of Billy Graham*	Beth Moore *President of Living Proof* & Sherron Watkins *Enron's "Whistle Blower"*	Kim Alexis & Debbye Turner *Supermodels*	Jody Eldred *Producer of Changed Lives: Miracles of The Passion of the Christ*	Yvette Maher *VP of Women's Ministry Focus on the Family*
LUNCHEON & HOST COMMITTEE CHAIRS				
Elizabeth Wareing	Audrey Holt Barbara McLaughlin Alice Peacock	Francie Willis	Linda Dunham Uldine Bisagno Jill McCleary Cheryl Thompson-Draper	Cindy Crane Garbs Bonnie Likover Cindy Walker
HONOREES				
Doris Morris	Marge Caldwell Jean "Mom" Caldwell Cathy Wining Thomas	Linda Dunham Dodie Osteen Martha Turner ~ Leonard Barksdale Bill Lawson Chuck Caldwell	Kay Arthur Donna Fujimoto Cole Gwenn Pierre Kim Watson ~ Gusta Booker David Self Remus Wright	Elisabeth Elliot Theola Booker Mary Ann Belin Francie Willis ~ "Secret Charlie"

Thank you to Joanie Haley of the McNair Foundation, Judy Aufman of Sweet Mercies Foundation, and Susan Silvus and Leslie Prokop of St. Luke's Methodist Church Outreach Council for encouraging us through our first grant requests. We will forever be grateful!

Leaders on the Host Committee
at the Inspire Women's Luncheon
Current And Past Years

Omana Abraham
Susan Arnoult
Molly Arp
Mary Beth Aspromonte
Chris Athon
Mary Attwell
Marcia Baker
Meredith Barineau
Pastor Leonard Barksdale
Stephanie Barron
Lisa Hale Bausbacher
Blair Belin
Mary Ann Belin
B. A. Bentsen
Gayle Bentsen
Dr. John & Uldine Bisagno
Collier Blades
Cindy Blanton
Theola Booker
Laurence Bragg
Linda Bratton
Melody Braun-Wilds
Lisa Brown Glenn
Lucia Bryan
Jeanette Burrell
Lezli Busbee
Carol Byrd
Jane Caldwell
Marge Caldwell
Lisa Calvert
Dougal & Cathy

Cameron
Myrna Cantu
Lucy Carl
Robert Carman
Melanie Cizik
Sue Coffey
Pamela Coleman
Madeline Collier
Allyson Cook
Jane Costello
Monica Crane
Beverly Cummings
Martha Curras
Shirley Dannenbaum
JoAnne Davis
Donna Dawson
Linda Dewhurst
April DiCecco
Paula Douglas
Linda Dunham
Marsha Eckermann
Lesha Elsenbrook
Diane Ender
Diana Fadrique
Carolyn Farb
Debbie Fiorito
Cathy Fitzpatrick
Barbara Forbes
Donna Fujimoto Cole
Mildred Ganchan
Cindy Crane Garbs
Nancy Gardner
Nan Garrett

George Gee
Harriett Gertner
Elizabeth Gillis
Donna Grehn
Shelley Haden
Joanie Haley
Janice Hall
Alberta Harris
Barbara Harris
Carol Harris
Nellwyn Harris
Suzanne Rhodes Hatcher
Wanda Jean Hickey
Karen Ho
Audrey Holt
Judy Horne
Elsie Huang
Barbara Hudson
Jennie Hull
Maxine Hull
Rebecca Hutcheson
Evelyn Jewell
Cathi Johansen
Fran Jolly
Julia Jordan
Donna Josey
Polly Kay
Malbie Kelly
Kathy Klein
Candy Knudson
Brenda Koch
Susan Lawhon

Leaders on the Host Committee
at the Inspire Women's Luncheon
Current And Past Years

Lesa Lawrence
Audrey Lawson
Tammy Leak
Beth Lee
Dana Lee
Pastor Johnnie Lee
Joy Levy
Stef Levy
Linda Ligon
Beverly Limestall Lindgren
Robin Livesay
Anita Marchione
Kelly Marchione
Marietta Maxfield
Meredith Maxfield Iler
Christina Reckling McConn
Linda McKechnie
Janice McNair
Linda McReynolds
Mary Catherine Miller
Leila Mischer
Patti Monroe
Kathy Munger
Cynthia Myers
Debbie Norris
Carolyn O'Neal
Anita O'Shaughnessy
Joyce Odom
Evelyn Ogletree
Nancy Jane Otto
Marianita Paddock
Diana Pardue

Debra Paxton
Alice Peacock
Helen Perry
Kathy Phillips
Lachelle Pierre
Doug & Puddie Pitcock
Cheryl Pitts-Bryant
Mary Leslie Plumhoff
Nancy Polis
Nancy Pressler
Rachel Quan
Natasha Rawson
Meg Rice
Bobbi Robinson
Cindy Rose
Shirley Ruiz
Danette Scheffler
Pam Schwab
Raquel Segal
Cecile Shannon
Lisa Simon
Sherry Smith
Fran Spector
Virginia Steppe
Gigi Strahan
Pat M. Sugarek
Madalyn Sykes
Lyndia Tarkington
Janet Taylor
Conte Terrell
Cheryl Thompson-Draper
Dotty Tompkins

Linda Toyota
Dawn Trozzo
Andrea Turtur
Carol Turtur
Byron Ubernosky
Bev Victory
Donna Walden
Cindy Walker
Rudyne Walker
Paula Walter
Lisa Ward
Elizabeth Wareing
Sherron Watkins
Kim Watson
Suzanne Watson
Bonnie Weekley
Sheretta West
Laura Wheless
Sue Whitfield
Patricia Williams
Gerry Williamson
Dawn Willis
Francie Willis
Lyndalin Willis
Mary Willis
Cathy Wining-Thomas
Karen Winston
Stacy Winston
Donna Wong
Bettina Wright
Jamie Wright
Mia Wright

Leaders Who Shared
Teaching, Music, or Drama
at the Inspire Women's Conference

Abiding Faith Baptist
"Angels of Praise"

Abundant Life Cathedral
"Word in Motion"

Ad Deum dance company

Kim Alexis

Kay Arthur

Kim Bady

Esmeralda Barrera

Jessie Berry

Monica Bilbo

Theola Booker &
Alita Corne Booker

Brentwood Baptist choir members

Mary Ann Bridgewater

Jill Briscoe

Brookhollow Baptist choir members

Brookhollow Praise dancers

Kathy Taylor Brown

Marge Caldwell

Suzette Caldwell

Damaris Carbaugh

Deborah Clifton

Jeannette Clift George

Donna Fujimoto Cole

Covenant Glen UMC choir members

Rozie Curtis

Shannon Cutts

Maria Darling

Gail Devers

Catalina Estrada

Lois Evans

Dr. Tony Evans

Priscilla Evans Shirer

Chrystal Evans-Hurst

Jody Eldred

Leona Ellis

Felicia Fontenot

Fountain of Praise choir members

Fountain of Praise Cross dancers

Maria Gabriella Garcia

Gloria Gaither &
Amy Gaither-Hayes

Barbara Harris Curtis

Greater St. Matthew choir members

Halleluiah praise dancers

Shirley Harrington

Magda Hermida

Houston's First Baptist
choir members

Inspire Women's multi-ethnic choir

Georgine Iloff

Sonny Messiah-Jiles

Leaders Who Shared
Teaching, Music, or Drama
at the Inspire Women's Conference

Zelda Johnson & Michelle Johnson

Joanne Juren

Eulalia King

Libo Krieg

Beverly Laubach

Sabrina Li

Keri Lilley

Pat Lilley

Lakewood choir members

Beverly Laubach

Audrey Lawson

Melanie Lawson

Living Proof worship team

Ambassador Halima Sirker Lopez

Linda Lorelle

Gloria Londono

Cheryl Martin

Dolly Martin

Lois McCall

Rosalyn Brunswick-McDuffie

Jeremy McCasland

Linda McKechnie

Ruth Graham McIntyre

Terri Miller

Saundra Montgomery

Beth Moore

Martha Moore

Susan O'Donnell

Carolyn O'Neal

Victoria Osteen

Out of Eden

Helen Perry

Carolyn Pickens

Lisa Pierre

Sharon Radionoff

Cindy Cruse Ratcliff

Meg Rice

Marlia Ruiz

Joy Shin

St. Luke's St Cecelia's choir

Charisse Strawberry

Isis Tuel

Indy Vormbrock

Cindy Walker

Sherron Watkins

Maxcine Watson

Sarah Welch

Sheretta West

Mia Wright

Jo Beth Young

Friends Who Helped to Grow
the Inspire Women's Organization

Hebrews 11:32, "And what more shall I say?
I do not have time to tell about..."

DONATED TIME & SERVICES	NAME OF INDIVIDUAL/MINISTRY/COMPANY
Prayer Coordinators	Carol Byrd ~ Denise Malloy ~ Mary Ann Bridgewater
Office Space	Dougal and Cathy Cameron
Website Design	Roy Urrego
Accounting Services	Byron Ubernosky, Ubernosky, Passmore, Majeres, LLP
Legal Advice	Jerry Walker ~ Lisa Brown ~ David Quan
Hardware configuration, Database design and administration	Mike Taylor ~ Debo Bartos ~ Gretchen Browning ~ Sheryll Roberson ~ Cynthia Myers ~ John Ju ~ Trisha Cook ~ Aly Teran ~ Erick Figueroa ~ Bob Schlesinger ~ Izzy Martinez ~ Ginger Martinez
Printing	Tad Molloy, Printing-X-Press ~ Barkla Tully, SW Precision Printing
Graphics Design	Chan Do, Machan Design ~ Jamie Wright, The Wright Touch ~ Linda Huang ~ Scott Reavis, Houston's First Baptist Church ~ Lee Bouldin, College of Biblical Studies
Marketing and Publicity	Linda Huang ~ Cynthia Stielow ~ Sandra Glahn, Dallas Seminary *Kindred Spirit* ~ Richard Vara, Houston Chronicle ~ Christian Events Magazine
Video/audio Production	Ginger and Martin Gaston, ENG Image Rachel Quan ~ Radkney Jolink, First Presbyterian Church of Houston ~ Gigi Strahan, Second Baptist Church Vic Mignona, Houston's First Baptist Church ~ Jerry Weaver, Sound on Tape
Event Production and Consultation	Gene Tow ~ Eulalia King ~ Debbie Blackwood ~ Cindy Crane Garbs ~ John Fosdick ~ Buck Anderson ~ Aimee Wilson ~ Rozie Curtis ~ Alberta Harris ~ Bobbi Robinson ~ Rachel Quan ~ Michelle Eustler
Radio/Television Time	Bruce Munstermann, Bonnie Bement, Dolly Martin, KHCB J.R. Hernandez, Susan O'Donnell, KSBJ ~ Ken Garza, KKHT ~ WB-39 News ~ KETH-TV ~ D'Andria Banks, KLTJ Daystar

Friends Who Helped to Grow
the Inspire Women's Organization

Hebrews 11:32, "And what more shall I say?
I do not have time to tell about..."

DONATED TIME & SERVICES	NAME OF INDIVIDUAL/MINISTRY/COMPANY
Florist	Sue Habib of Lexis Florist ~
	Elaine Ousley-Nevarez of Elaine's Florist
Postal services/ Packing materials/Delivery	International Mailing Systems
	Marcy Malloy, Action Box
	Carl Grijalba
Photography	Alvin Gee Photographers ~ John Leech ~ Kim Koffman
Office Setup and Telecommunications	Mike Taylor ~ John Howell ~ Cass Davies ~ Gretchen Browning ~ Earl Morrison ~ Craig Girdnt ~ Freddy ~ The VIA Group ~ VDI ~ Robert Polis ~ Robbie Carman ~ Thomas Carman
Top Recruiters	Victoria Schlesinger ~ Karen McCord ~ Deela Roe ~ Lyndia Tarkington ~ Antoinette Bell ~ Jerrilynne Robertson ~ Esmeralda Barrera ~Izzy Martinez ~ Gladys Fadden ~ Lily Da Silva ~ Libo Krieg
Year-round Helping Hands	Gretchen Browning ~ Kristina Hunt ~ Dick Linggo Lucy Linggo ~ Karen McCord ~ Sheryll Roberson

Photographs

Tears being shed as Anita recalls past memories

Anita in her single days

Anita (age2) with Dad

Anita in her 2nd Grade
school uniform

Anita's mother

Bobby, Rosita, Anita and Mom

Anita (age 2) and Rosita (age 4)

Anita and Rosita praying

Rosita and Anita with their mother
on their apartment rooftop

Thomas, Anita and Robbie

Inspire Women's sponsored event

Anita teaching at Inspire Women's Conference

Dr. Mark Bailey, President of Dallas Theological Seminary,
presents Anita with her degree

Anita with her nearly 80 year old father
who volunteers every week at Inspire Women

A Personal

Reflection Journal

For You to discover
where Your new story begins

(Condensed from the original bible study,
"When Dreams Won't Die")

Foreword To Personal Reflection Journal

Years ago, I read an article differentiating intelligence quotient (I.Q.) and emotional quotient (E.Q.). The point the article made was that no matter how intelligent we are, our potential will be hindered if we have a low emotional quotient. Our emotional quotient is what shapes what we believe about ourselves. As I was writing this autobiography, God impressed on my heart that I needed to add a personal reflection supplement. This supplement is an excerpt from a work I originally compiled years ago, titled "When Dreams Won't Die." In this foreword, let me explain the purpose for this supplement.

There are many wonderful materials other great teachers have written that will help you discover God's vision for your life. There are even workbooks and seminars that will help you implement a God-sized dream. However, I have found that you can help someone discover their gifts and God's vision for their lives but they will not use their gifts nor step into God's dream until some fundamentals are taken care of. I believe these fundamentals will shape your emotional quotient and what you believe God can and will do through you.

In this supplemental personal reflection journal, what God led me to share are the truths that took me out of the prison of my own mind to stepping into God's imaginations for my life. In the lesson on how to soar from a heritage of greatness, I pray you will step into your eternal family tree and learn from a God who had the courage to repair a dream. In the lesson on how to let go of the past, I pray you will no longer live in the world of "what if's" or "what could have been's" and begin to live in the world of "Even if…" In spite of all that has happened that may have broken your heart, will you follow God into a future adventure and experience His miraculous power? In the lesson of celebrating with God into the future, I pray you will never allow fear to limit you. I pray that you will be compelled with a confidence in the God who is the author and finisher of our faith. When we allow God to write the end of our stories, we can have the assurance that everything God's hand touches ends with the words, "It is good. It is very good."

PART I

Soar From A Heritage of Greatness

I still remember the day when I left Hong Kong. I was seventeen. Less than six months before my departure, my mother had taken her own life. I had my ticket in my hands, all my life belongings in two suitcases, and my nineteen year old sister beside me, as we marched bravely onto the aircraft.

This was the day we all dreamed about but we never expected the dream to be fulfilled in this way. We thought the whole family would leave on an immigration visa. Instead, my parent's petition to enter America was denied and my sister and I were leaving on a student visa, granted us based on our academic achievement and the full scholarships we had been awarded from an American university.

Many times, life does not materialize the way we envision it. For my family, we did not expect that our mother, the woman who believed in the impossible dream of America for her family, would somehow lose the dream for herself. We did not expect that we would wave good-bye to our father and leave him standing at the gate, shriveled and defeated by the loss of all his loved ones in such a short time.

As the plane lifted off the land where I was born, I quietly wrapped my arms around myself, acting brave on the outside but feeling my personal world crumbling on the inside. Have you ever felt life moving on, like a conveyor belt, while you are standing still? Have you ever felt like you have lost all control of what might happen and your only hope is that there is a God, that He is good, that He has your life in His hands, and that He knows where He is going?

For quite some time after I arrived in the Promise Land, I wandered around in a daze. Who are you when no one knows who you are? Who are you when there is no family structure around you or friends to remind you of your character, your potential, your past successes or failures? Who are you when your name means nothing because no one knows your family, your roots, your history? For the first time in my life, I was it; and I had to find out for myself what I was all about.

What is Your Name?

Imagine yourself as the only survivor of a plane crash that put you in the middle of nowhere. You find yourself waking up, staring into the faces of a primitive people who neither speak your language nor understand your culture. Here, stripped of your titles and the people relationships that once defined you, I want you to ask yourself, "Who am I? What is my name and what does that name stand for?"

MY ANSWER:
_____
_____
_____
_____

In the Hebrew culture, once a thing is named, it is defined. In Ephesians chapter 3, verse 12-15, the apostle Paul said, "In him and through faith in him we may approach God with freedom and confidence ... For this reason, I kneel before the Father, from whom his whole family in heaven and on earth derives its name."

According to Ephesians 3:15, where do we get our name?

MY ANSWER:

_____

_____

_____

_____

What emotion does bearing this name evoke in the Apostle Paul?

MY ANSWER:

_____

_____

_____

What made it possible for us to receive this name?

MY ANSWER:

_____

_____

_____

_____

What does bearing God's name mean to you?

MY ANSWER:

_____

_____

_____

_____

It is my utmost conviction that the reason for our lack of power in Christian living comes from our lack of identity. Do you really understand what it means to bear your Father's name? Let me put it this way. How do you hold yourself when you walk into a room? Where do you find your confidence? Is it in your accomplishments, in whether someone has chosen to love or reject you, in your appearance, in your wealth? How permanent are these building materials? If your confidence rests in these things, then your confidence is but an illusion. How can we expect to operate with power when the foundation of our lives is pre-dictably collapsible? It is on God's Word that God wants to build your life and mine. May I share with you what God taught me about bearing His name?

Paul tells us that we derive our name from the Father. In other words, if Jesus is God's first name and Christ is God's last name, your last name is now Christ. Try it on for size. My name is Anita Christ. What is your name?

Now, that may sound strange or it may even sound good to you but the name itself has no meaning if you do not understand the significance of the "Christ" name. For example, if I was a homeless bum and found out that I was the child that Mr. Rockefeller has been searching for, that reality would have no significance if I didn't know what the Rockefeller name stood for. I would still walk around like a bum; I would still have the counte-nance of a homeless and insignificant bum. But if I knew that the Rockefeller name stood for prestige and tremendous wealth, my countenance would immediately change and I would run like the wind to my father, Mr. Rockefeller, and celebrate my new found identity and all the perks that come with my new name.

I remember when my son was ten; I asked him, "What if Abraham Lincoln was in your family tree?" His eyes got very big and he said, "O-oh, I would be so proud." I asked him, "Would you live differently?" He said, "Of course. I would try to be better than my best." But what would he have said if he never took American history and had no idea who Abraham Lincoln was? Do you see how being related to a great man would have absolutely no sig-nificance in his life?

When God's Dream for us First Began

The Apostle Paul understood the significance of having his name derived from the Father. How do I know? Because Paul began his statement with "For this reason". He is referring to the reason why he is in awe and kneels before the Father. So we must ask ourselves, "For what reason?"

The Apostle Paul summarizes his reason in a nutshell in the words "In him and through faith in him we may approach God with freedom and confidence." Therefore it is for this reason that Paul is in awe of God's name. So now, we have another problem, what in the world does "In him and through faith in him ..." mean? So much background is wrapped up in those words that unless we take the time to understand the fullness of this statement, the truth revealed in these words flies right over our heads. When Paul says, "In him ..." he is referring to what God has done. It was something God did that made it possible for us to bear His name. We cannot possibly appreciate the full significance of our name until we fully appreciate what God had to do.

If I were to tell you my family's story and said, "The Lie Family immigrated from Hong Kong to the United States." you would not begin to understand the impact of my statement unless you had been there when the dream first began in my family's heart. You would not experience the deep emotions unless you had walked with me through those years: the glimmer of possibility, the hope, the trials, the setbacks, the perseverance, the patience, the heartache, the high price of the death of a family member. You would not be able to experience the full impact of my current reality unless you were aware of my family's heritage and background.

In the same way, you cannot fully appreciate your heavenly Father's name until you understand your heavenly family's heritage and history. So, I am going to take you back to when God's dream for His children first began.

Study the following verses from Genesis, chapter 1. What repeated adjective did God use to describe what He had created? How many times did God use the same adjective?

Gen 1:10 God called the dry ground "land," and the gathered waters he called "seas." And God saw that it was good.

Gen 1:12 The land produced vegetation: plants bearing seed according to their kinds and trees bearing fruit with seed in it according to their kinds. And God saw that it was good.

Gen 1:16-18 God made two great lights– the greater light to govern the day and the lesser light to govern the night. He also made the stars. God set them in the expanse of the sky to give light on the earth, to govern the day and the night, and to separate light from darkness. And God saw that it was good.

Gen 1:21 So God created the great creatures of the sea and every living and moving thing with which the water teems, according to their kinds, and every winged bird according to its kind. And God saw that it was good.

Gen 1:25 God made the wild animals according to their kinds, the livestock according to their kinds, and all the creatures that move along the ground according to their kinds. And God saw that it was good.

Gen 1:31 God saw all that he had made, and it was very good. And there was evening, and there was morning– the sixth day.

MY ANSWER:

_____

_____

_____

_____

In "Disappointment with God," Philip Yancey put it this way: "And God saw that it was good" – five times the understatement beats in cadence like a drum. And when he had finished, "God saw all that he had made, and it was very good."[1]

God gave His children one command:

Gen 2:16-17 And the LORD God commanded the man, "You are free to eat from any tree in the garden; but you must not eat from the tree of the knowledge of good and evil, for when you eat of it you will surely die."

What was God's command?

MY ANSWER:
_____
_____
_____
_____

What are the adjectives describing the forbidden tree?

MY ANSWER:
_____
_____
_____
_____

What do you think is the significance of eating from a tree described as having "the knowledge of good and evil"? Would it have made any difference if the tree was described as something else, had different characteristics? Was it just any tree and God was simply wanting our obedience or was God particularly and specifically interested in this tree because of what it stood for?

MY ANSWER:
_____
_____
_____
_____

Have you ever asked yourself, "What exactly did Adam and Eve hope to obtain by eating the forbidden fruit?" Did you notice that the tree was described as having the "knowledge of good and evil"? Now think for a moment. What is often our greatest spiritual struggle? James Dobson in his book, "When God Doesn't Make Sense", said, "The human spirit is capable of withstanding enormous discomfort, including the prospect of death, if the circumstances make sense. Many martyrs, political prisoners, and war heroes have gone to their graves willingly and confidently."[2]

In other words, it is not so much the suffering that we mind but it is when we suffer and cannot see a good reason for it. Now, do you see the significance in the tree of the knowledge of good and evil? From the beginning of time, we have struggled with God over what makes sense, what we determine to be good and worthwhile, and what we have concluded to be evil. When God told Adam and Eve not to eat of the tree of the knowledge of good and evil, God was reserving the right to decide what is good and bad in our lives. In a nutshell, God wants to decide. The question is, "Will you let Him?" What is holding you back from allowing God to be Lord and Master of your life?

MY ANSWER:

_____

_____

_____

_____

Let's return to the scene in the Garden of Eden. Satan approaches God's children and says:

> **Gen 3:1-6** ... "Did God really say, 'You must not eat from any tree in the garden'? ... "You will not surely die ... For God knows that when you eat of it your eyes will be opened, and you will be like God, knowing good and evil."

And God watched the heart of His children turn against Him. They took the fruit and ate it. As a parent, I want you to imagine yourself in a room with one of those mirrors where you can see your children but they can't see you. You are watching as someone has entered that room and is talking your kids into doing something you have adamantly instructed them against. You hear the lies and you watch the deceit going down. What is going on inside you? Do you find yourself praying, hoping that they will remember, that they will hold on to the wisdom you have tried to pour into their lives? Can you almost hear God cry out, "Oh Adam, oh Eve, choose life. Choose life, my children, for that is what your heavenly Father is all about. From the overflowing life in your Father, He created the world. Choose life, Adam. Choose life, Eve. That is your heritage." But Adam and Eve chose death and in their choice, they were separated eternally from the Father.

Feeling God's Anguish
When We Chose Against Him

When I served as a leader in Beth Moore's Sunday School class, God led me to write a Christmas play titled "God's War Cry". So many of the women were going through a difficult time and I asked God for a fresh way for the class to experience Christmas. The class produced "God's War Cry". The significance of the title is seen at the end of the play when the war trumpets sound, and God's battle cry resounds through the world with the infant cry of baby Jesus. The following verses inspired the words to Acts two of "God's War Cry" in which Satan had a major confrontation with God over what happened in Eden.

Study Psalms 56:8 and then answer the following questions.

Ps 56:8 Record my lament; list my tears on your scroll– are they not in your record?

What does God keep track of?

MY ANSWER:
_____
_____
_____
_____
_____

What do you keep track of in your relationship with a loved one?

MY ANSWER:
_____
_____
_____
_____

How would your relationships change if you felt the pain of your loved one more than you felt the wrong they committed against you?

MY ANSWER:

_____

_____

_____

Study the verses in 2 Samuel 12:7-8 and then answer the following questions.

> **2 Sam 12:7-8** ... I anointed you king over Israel, and I delivered you from the hand of Saul. I gave your master's house to you, and your master's wives into your arms. I gave you the house of Israel and Judah. And if all this had been too little, I would have given you even more.

God reminded David of his past, before accusing him of not trusting. Take some time to record what God has done for you. God has a track record of coming through. How does remembering what He has done help you to trust Him with your future?

MY ANSWER:

_____

_____

_____

In spite of all that God had given David, what did God say He would have been willing to do?

MY ANSWER:

_____

_____

_____

How are you satisfying the hunger in your life? Have you given up on God? How are you finding your own solutions?

MY ANSWER:

_____

_____

_____

_____

According to the verses in Hosea, listed below, what memories was God referring to?

> **Hosea 11:3-4** It was I who taught Ephraim to walk, taking them by the arms; but they did not realize it was I who healed them. I led them with cords of human kindness, with ties of love; I lifted the yoke from their neck and bent down to feed them.

> **Hosea 11:8** "How can I give you up, Ephraim? How can I hand you over, Israel? How can I treat you like Admah? How can I make you like Zeboiim? My heart is changed within me; all my compassion is aroused.

MY ANSWER:

_____

_____

_____

Sometimes, as God establishes us, we become demanding and ungrateful and expect things from God as if He owes us something. Have you grown too big for your britches? When was the last time you praised God? Name some ways success may lead you away from God? What successes has God given you that might have caused you to grow arrogant and cold toward Him?

MY ANSWER:

_____

_____

_____

Yet, notice God's response in spite of us. How does knowing this character about your Father affect your attitude?

MY ANSWER:

_____

_____

_____

_____

Study the verses in Genesis 6:6-7 and answer the following questions.

Gen 6:6-7 The LORD was grieved that he had made man on the earth, and his heart was filled with pain. So the LORD said, "I will wipe mankind, whom I have created, from the face of the earth– men and animals, and creatures that move along the ground, and birds of the air– for I am grieved that I have made them."

So often, we focus on our disappointment with God. Has it ever occurred to you that sometimes, God too might be disappointed? What words express God's disappointment? What did God want to do?

MY ANSWER:

_____

_____

_____

Now, let me share with you the words of Act 2 in "God's Warcry". Imagine Satan strutting into the presence of God, defiant and disrespectful. Satan is peachy pleased with himself. God is in the middle of penning in His scroll: He records the tears of His children, as they begin to suffer the irreversible consequences of their choice.

SATAN

They'll miss you, but they'll get over it.

GOD

No, they won't. They weren't made in your image. They were made in mine and born from my heart. Without me, they will never find their rest.

SATAN

Isn't that too bad? You will always know that they are with me and miserable!

(No one speaks. Then Satan starts up again.)

If you ask me, God, you had a very major design flaw. You see, you gave the children free will and that was your first mistake.

GOD

No, Satan, love is never a mistake. I made them a son, not a slave, and as a son, I gave them free will.

SATAN

Free will to choose against you! I think you would have been better not giving them any will at all!

GOD

You're wrong. Not give them free will? How could it have been better to love them less?

SATAN

I sympathize with your dilemma and now, your pain. But I think, I've won. Do you concede?

GOD

Never! They are mine! No one will snatch them out of my hands.

SATAN

Fine! You can look at them then through the bars of their cages but you'll never be able to hold them. They have no power to cross over from the prison of their fallenness into your loving arms.

GOD

Then I will go and get them.

SATAN

Get them? They are fallen flesh! Your burning righteousness will consume their sin in your very presence. So, perhaps you will go and get them but how will you have them, without destroying them in the process? Seems to me, you have a problem.

GOD

And it's my problem, isn't it? Now get out of my sight!

(Satan exits. In the silence of His chambers, God expresses His deep sorrow.)

GOD

My children, you want to be free, but freedom is only found in me. Once, you were so secure in my arms and your heart cried out, "Daddy, I love you." But you chose to go away and the song in my heart, it died today, with you. Why, my children, why? I lifted you from the dust and breathed my royalty into your veins. I gave you the world for your celebration and if that had been too little, I would have given you even more. Why did you despise my word by doing what is evil in my sight? Now, look at you, your royal countenance distorted with fear and despair. Your regal form disintegrating into death. Did I not tell you? Did I not warn you? Why? Why? Why?

(God rips up the scroll, falls on his knees, and weeps.)

END OF ACT TWO

God's Courage to Dream Again

Do you think God ever gets disappointed? Do you think He ever wants to rip up the canvas on which He painted His masterpiece? Does he ever say, "I wish I never had kids!"

Yet, God did not wipe humankind from the face of the earth. Though he was forced to rip up the first canvas, He had the courage to dream again.

John 3:16 "For God so loved the world that he gave his one and only Son, that whoever believes in him shall not perish but have eternal life.

In John 3:16, what emotion was greater in God than His sorrow over our sin?

MY ANSWER:

_____

_____

_____

_____

Can you describe a time in your life when love held your hand and was stronger than your emotion to lash out in vengeance?

MY ANSWER:

_____

_____

_____

_____

God "so loved the world" that "he gave his one and only son": God's love was greater than His sorrow. God was able to release His son to death because He chose for His emotion of love for all His children to be greater than the sorrow of giving up His one and only son. Have you ever had to release a loved one to death? Have you ever lost something close to your heart such as your business or your house? What is your greatest treasure? Can you give God your most precious possession? Will you allow your love for God to be greater than the sorrow of your loss? If so, can you write down the treasure you are placing at the feet of God as your love offering.

MY ANSWER:

_____

_____

_____

_____

When I was a little girl, I remember watching my mother when she was praying. I remember the lines of longing in her face, how she desired with all her heart to live in the free land of America. I saw the glimmer oh hope in her eyes when we filed our papers requesting immigration to America. I saw the deep lines of disappointment when our first petition was refused. I saw anguish in her soul and with all my heart, I wanted to fulfill her dream for her. Because of my background, when I read God's Word, I can feel His heart and sometimes, I wonder, "Did my Lord Jesus lean up against His Father? Did He watch His Father's face? Did He long to fulfill the Father's dream? Did He say, 'Father, send me.'" And Jesus, "who, being in very nature God, did not consider equality with God something to be grasped, but made himself nothing, taking the very nature of a servant, being made in human likeness. And being found in appearance as a man, he humbled himself and became obedient to death– even death on a cross!" (Phil 2:6-8)

What price did God pay for our redemption? How does knowing what God was willing to give up transform your attitude over what you may have lost in life?

MY ANSWER:

_____

_____

_____

_____

Though the dream began in my mother's heart, she never made it to the Promise Land of America. She was the one who pleaded daily with God for the future of her children. She was the one who, in spite of not having a formal education herself, was able to train up her children in discipline and in academic excellence so that all three of her children were awarded full scholarships to American universities. Shortly before my sister and I were scheduled to leave, she entered into a deep depression. I will never know what was going through her mind. Now that God had opened a path for her children, did she think her role was over? Was the thought of perhaps never seeing us again too much for her? When she received news that her own petition to enter the United States was denied, did she lose hope that she would ever reach the Promise Land? I don't know. I will never know. But on that morning, when the shrill cry of my father shook me from my sleep, I woke up to find that my mother had hung herself from the rafters.

The Price of a Dream

When I received my American citizenship, there was a group of school children who came to sing the national anthem. Some had their shirt tails hanging out, some were chewing gum ... I grieved over their casual attitude and I thought, "You don't understand your heritage. You don't understand the price of freedom." As tears streamed down my face, I said, "Mom, I have it. I got your dream for you."

Oh Faithful One, read with me God's words in John 3:16:

John 3:16 "For God so loved the world that he gave his one and only Son, that whoever believes in him shall not perish but have eternal life.

What price did God pay to restore His dream for us? How does knowing what God was willing to do to protect your future affect how you respond to your life today?

MY ANSWER: _____

_____

_____

_____

On Calvary, God died so His dream for us could live. Faithful One, what price are you willing to pay for your dream? A dream worth living for is a dream worth dying for.

A few days before July 1, 1997, the historic day when Hong Kong as a British colony ceased to exist and Communist China marched in and raised her flag, I called my Dad and asked him how he felt. He said, "This was the day we dreaded. To think that all the family has made it to the United States fills my heart with gratitude to our Lord. All I can say is that the road to freedom was not strewn with rose petals."

Oh Faithful One, don't you see? All dreams have a price and God's dream for us had the greatest price of all. The road to our freedom was paid in full with the blood of God's one and only son. A just God could not leave sin unpunished. A loving God would not allow us to pay the penalty of sin. Jesus did not have to stay on that cross. He said about his life in John 10:18, "No one takes it from me, but I lay it down of my own accord. I have authority to lay it down and authority to take it up again ..." God stayed on that cross because God chose to die so we could live.

Faithful One, do you know what your name stands for? Your name was born from your Father's heart. You come from an eternal Father who had the courage to dream again and the stubborn love to pay the price for that dream to come true. Bearing His name is not something that just happened by chance. You were born from a heritage of greatness, of courage, of perseverance, of setback that was overturned, of a relentless love that refused to lose you. No one will snatch us out of our Father's hands.

I kneel before my Father from whom all heaven and earth derives its name. My name is Anita Christ. What is your name? How will bearing His name make a difference in your life?

PART II

❦

Leave the Past Behind Us

The day before my mother died, I was in my room doing my homework. Suddenly, I felt her presence and looked around to find her standing at the door to my bedroom. I was irritated because she had startled me and distracted me from my work. She said, "Just tell me that you don't need me anymore." That question hit me from left field. Without thinking, I said abruptly, "I don't need you anymore."

When I woke up the next day to find that she had taken her life I realized that I was the youngest, her baby. When she asked me that question, it was her way of saying, "I just need to know that my baby will be all right." In my abrupt answer, I had given her the permission to take her own life.

Describe an event you felt was your fault but you no longer have an opportunity to make things right.

MY ANSWER:

_____

_____

_____

_____

The Bondage of Past Sin

One of the leaders in my class once said to me, "The reason

why nothing is happening in my life is because God is displeased with me. He is punishing me for my past." What she didn't realize was that these were words repeated by several of my leaders and many of the members in my class. Somehow, Satan has deceived us into thinking that we have disqualified ourselves. We believe the lie that God could not possibly appoint us to any position of significance in His kingdom.

In the following verses, listed below, what past sin did Paul commit?

> **Acts 22:3-5** "I am a Jew, born in Tarsus of Cilicia, but brought up in this city. Under Gamaliel I was thoroughly trained in the law of our fathers and was just as zealous for God as any of you are today. I persecuted the followers of this Way to their death, arresting both men and women and throwing them into prison, as also the high priest and all the Council can testify. I even obtained letters from them to their brothers in Damascus, and went there to bring these people as prisoners to Jerusalem to be punished.

> **1 Tim 1:15** Here is a trustworthy saying that deserves full acceptance: Christ Jesus came into the world to save sinners– of whom I am the worst.

MY ANSWER: _____

_____

_____

_____

_____

In the following verses, what did Paul say compels him in his life? Do you think there is a relation between Paul's past and his momentum in his ministry?

> **2 Cor 5:14-15** For Christ's love compels us, because we are convinced that one died for all, and therefore all died. And he died for all, that those who live should no longer live for themselves but for him who died for them and was raised again.

MY ANSWER:
_____

_____

_____

Notice that Paul was guilty of murder. He was the one who persecuted the followers of Christ. Imagine how Paul must have felt after his conversion. As he ministered to the people in the name of Christ, he had to face the relatives of those he had killed. God did not choose to keep the past from staring him in the face. Yet, instead of allowing his past to cause him to feel inadequate in his ministry, Paul used his past as his spring board into a greater ministry. It was because he was the greater sinner that he embraced the grace of Christ all the more. It was because he needed more grace that he appreciated and was compelled in his life by the love of Christ. Faithful One, in your calling, how has God required you to walk back into the past from which you came?

MY ANSWER:
_____

_____

_____

In the following verses of Luke 7, listed below, what did Jesus teach about someone with greater sin?

Luke 7:37-38 When a woman who had lived a sinful life in that town learned that Jesus was eating at the Pharisee's house, she brought an alabaster jar of perfume, and as she stood behind him at his feet weeping, she began to wet his feet with her tears. Then she wiped them with her hair, kissed them and poured perfume on them.

Luke 7:44-47 Then he turned toward the woman and said to Simon, "Do you see this woman? I came into your house. You did not give me any water for my feet, but she wet my feet with her tears and wiped them with her hair. You did not give me a kiss, but this woman, from the time I entered, has not stopped kissing my feet. You did not put oil on my head, but she has poured perfume on my feet. Therefore, I tell you, her many sins have been forgiven– for she loved much. But he who has been forgiven little loves little."

MY ANSWER:

_____

_____

_____

Notice that Jesus said, "...he who has been forgiven little loves little." Oh Faithful One, some of us do not expect to hear from God because we are convinced our past sin has disqualified us from His service. The lie of Satan is to cripple us for the future because of a past failure. The truth of God is that a broken past gives us all the more reason to celebrate our new life in Christ. Past confessed sin is never the excuse for a lesser ministry. It is the catalyst for a greater one.

Have you been running away from your past? Did you know that God always walks through the Red Sea, not around it? This does not mean walking back into the lives of people who have hurt you and will continue to hurt you. It means not running from the fact that you have been hurt and allowing God to transform your pain into a blessing for others. When we disconnect ourselves from the past, we disconnect ourselves from the story God wants to tell through our lives. He is the one who transforms history. God is not afraid of your past. It is in our weakness that His power will be revealed. Do you believe this? What is keeping you from receiving this truth for your life?

MY ANSWER:

_____

_____

_____

_____

The Regret of "If-Only"

Faithful One, are you haunted by all the "if-only's" in your life, things you could have said or could have done, words you wish you could take back? Satan wants to keep us paralyzed in the world of "if-only". Instead, God knows that we are imperfect. For that reason, He sent His son into the world. Perhaps, instead of living the blame game, we can come before the cross and thank our God for dying for our imperfections.

The Apostle understood the grace of God. Study the verses in Philippians 3, listed below, and answer the following questions:

Phil 3:12-14 Not that I have already obtained all this, or have already been made perfect, but I press on to take hold of that for which Christ Jesus took hold of me. Brothers, I do not consider myself yet to have taken hold of it. But one thing I do: Forgetting what is behind and straining toward what is ahead, I press on toward the goal to win the prize for which God has called me heavenward in Christ Jesus.

What did Jesus take hold of us for?

MY ANSWER:

_____

_____

_____

Jesus did not die on the cross so that we can continue to live in the bondage of our past. Christ Jesus came to set us free. How free is your life? What is keeping you from walking in freedom with God into the future?

MY ANSWER:

_____

_____

_____

_____

What did Paul say he was going to forget? Can you see how dwelling on the past (either past failures or past successes) can stunt our pace and keep us from moving forward?

MY ANSWER:

God's mercies are renewed everyday. Imagine the slate of your life as a blank clean slate. God is offering you the miracle of a new beginning. You have the opportunity to pen a brand new chapter in your life. Imagine today as the first day of the rest of your life. What do you want to do?

MY ANSWER:

Making Peace with What Could Have Happened But Didn't

The afternoon after my mother died, my neighbor came over and said, "Why didn't you call me? I am a nurse. I might have been able to revive her with CPR." In life, we hear of so many stories when God intervened miraculously. Yet, in our situation, God did not intervene. How do you go on with life knowing that God could have done something but He didn't?

Faithful One, this is a question we must settle. Unless we settle it, we cannot move with God into the future. Light has no fellowship with darkness. In the same way, mistrust has no fellowship with trust. To walk with God totally and unreservedly, we must trust God.

In John 11 verses 1-6, why did God not intervene as quickly as Mary and Martha would have desired. Why did God delay?

John 11:1-6 Now a man named Lazarus was sick. He was from Bethany, the village of Mary and her sister Martha. This Mary, whose brother Lazarus now lay sick, was the same one who poured perfume on the Lord and wiped his feet with her hair. So the sisters sent word to Jesus, "Lord, the one you love is sick." When he heard this, Jesus said, "This sickness will not end in death. No, it is for God's glory so that God's Son may be glorified through it." Jesus loved Martha and her sister and Lazarus. Yet when he heard that Lazarus was sick, he stayed where he was two more days. NIV

MY ANSWER:

In the beginning of John 11:21, what was Martha's accusation? Do you see any similarities in what you have said to God?

John 11:21 "Lord," Martha said to Jesus, "if you had been here, my brother would not have died.

MY ANSWER:

In John 11:22, Martha transitioned from accusation to faith. She said, "But I know that even now..." What about you? Are you stuck in accusation or can you complete the sentence, "But God, even now considering what has happened, I will..." How have you chosen to trust God in spite of the circumstances?

John 11:21-22 "Lord," Martha said to Jesus, "if you had been here, my brother would not have died. But I know that even now God will give you whatever you ask."

MY ANSWER:

_____

_____

_____

After Jesus heard of Lazarus' illness, He "stayed where he was two more days". In other words, God deliberately delayed. Notice how we often respond to God's absence with accusations. We say to God, "If you had been here ..." We say this because we expect life to work out a certain way and we are annoyed when God changes our plan. Sometimes, we even resent God for not coming through for us. After all, isn't He here to do our bidding? So, we begin to feel deceived by God. We echo the crowd who said in John 11:37, "Could not he who opened the eyes of the blind man have kept this man from dying?" In other words, "God, if you are as great as you say you are, then why haven't you come through for me?" Some of us even put God on a timeline and find ourselves saying, "All right, I haven't given up on you yet. I'm giving you another chance to come through!"

In spite of us, God moves in such a way to reveal His power. Lazarus was four days in the tomb so that God could demonstrate His power over death. "Lazarus, come out!" were words spoken by God to show that one word from the mouth of the creator and new life erupts from the ashes. Oh Faithful One, if you find yourself in the pit of despair, please know that God's story never ends with death. God's story ends with the resurrection. All our life stories echo the one story closest to God's heart. Your life is but another way God chooses tell the world that He is in the business of resurrecting life out of death. What comfort does it give you knowing how God has already written your story to end in victory?

MY ANSWER:

_____
_____
_____
_____
_____
_____

Closing the Chapter, Turning the Page

After the loss of my mother, many caring people tried to help me with my grief by saying, "This is the end of a chapter in your life. Now turn the page and go on." Those words were easier said than done. The problem was, I had an emotional gaping hole in my heart. How does one go on in life with a hole in one's heart?

How does the truth in Galatians 2:20 help you put your past to rest?

> **Gal 2:20** I have been crucified with Christ and I no longer live, but Christ lives in me. The life I live in the body, I live by faith in the Son of God, who loved me and gave himself for me.

MY ANSWER:

_____
_____
_____
_____
_____

List the hurtful events and injustices in your past that you are still carrying around with you. Now, imagine nailing this past to the cross and allowing Jesus to pay the penalty for the wrong that you did and all the wrong that was committed against you. If your past was truly crucified as Paul's was, you would walk as Paul did with the new life of Christ in him. Faithful One, what might be keeping you from leaving your past crucified to the cross?

MY ANSWER:

_____

_____

_____

_____

God is Satisfied.
The Question Is, "Are You?"

On Calvary, Jesus cried out, "It is finished." On Calvary, the blood of Jesus paid the full penalty of every sin past, present, and future. The blood of Jesus paid for those sins you committed as well as those sins committed against you. On Calvary, God was satisfied. The question is, "Are you?"

MY ANSWER:

_____

_____

_____

After my mother's death, we found her most expensive pieces of jewelry missing. As the family tried to piece together the events that led to her death, we concluded that she had sold the jewelry as some kind of peace offering. Somehow, during her last days, she was deceived into believing that God was holding a grudge against her, that perhaps God had a curse on her life because of her past. Therefore, she was trying to make peace with God. In her confusion, I think she also gave up her life as a peace offering, thinking that her sacrifice would remove the curse from her family and win God's favor for her children.

This may sound bizarre to you and yet, I have met so many believers who respond to their trials with a similar mentality. They are convinced that God is withholding His blessing, that because of past sin, God's wrath would follow them all of their lives. Nothing is further from the truth. God's wrath was completely satisfied on Calvary.

A year and a half after my mother's death, my brother had re-petitioned the U.S. government and my father was granted entrance into the United States. That blessing would have belonged to my mother as well, if only she had kept her faith, a little longer. God had prepared a feast for her but she had believed Satan's lie instead of trusting in her Father's heart.

Oh Faithful One, God created us to be subduers and overcomers and God's calling is irrevocable. With Calvary, Jesus returned to us the power to be rulers on this earth over the prince of darkness. Sin has no power over us. Death has lost its sting. When Jesus cried out, "It is finished", the bondage of sin was broken and life on planet earth was transformed, reversed, and restored to the way God intended when He first made us.

Jesus cried out, "It is finished" and God is satisfied. What about you? Is there something you need to finish in your life? What are you having trouble forgiving yourself for?

MY ANSWER:

_____

_____

_____

_____

_____

_____

List the names of those you have trouble forgiving. Now, imagine God giving them the same punishment as He allowed Jesus to endure. Are you satisfied with Calvary's sacrifice? If not, how much more must our Savior suffer before you are satisfied that the price of sin has been paid for in full? How many more lashes will it take on Jesus' back? How many more nails will it take in Jesus' hands before you are satisfied that the full penalty of sin was paid on Calvary?

MY ANSWER:

_____
_____
_____
_____
_____
_____
_____

Oh Faithful One, God has restored us for celebration. Please don't live in the prison of your yesterdays but allow God to transform your history to reveal His power in our weakness. "It is finished!" Oh may that declaration sink it. May we receive it as God's invitation to leave the past behind and to transform our history for the dream God has for our lives. In these words that our Lord cried out from Calvary, may we find the freedom to walk with God into a royal future.

PART III

Celebrate with God into Your Future

Someone once said to me, "Dreams are like air castles. They vanish in thin air." I disagree. Sometimes, I wish dreams could be buried but the problem with dreams is that they never die. The hope of their fulfillment may be over but somehow, the desire for the dream lives on in our hearts. What do you do with a dream that has no possibility of becoming a reality? How do you take a dream that refuses to die and find new hope for the future?

And the Earth was Formless and Void

The good news is, we come from a heritage of a heavenly Father who had a dream for us and refused to let His dream die. Our heavenly Father breathed His Spirit into us. Therefore, we have the Spirit of one who persevered in spite of setbacks, who had the stubborn love and the courage to rebuild a new dream.

In the verses of Genesis 1, listed below, what was the role of God's Holy Spirit?

Gen 1:1 In the beginning God created the heavens and the earth.

Gen 1:2 And the earth was formless and void, and darkness was over the surface of the deep; and the Spirit of God was moving over the surface of the waters.

MY ANSWER:

_____

_____

_____

_____

_____

In Hebrew, numbers can be singular, dual, or plural (meaning more than two). In Genesis 1:1, the word for God is in the plural form.[1] In other words, not only were God the Father and God the Son present but a third person was also present at the beginning when God created the heavens and the earth.

In Genesis 1:2, we see that the one contributing to the "more than two" plural form in Genesis 1:1 is God's Holy Spirit because God's Word says. "the Spirit of God was moving over the surface of the waters." This tells me that God's Holy Spirit is involved with creation. He is able to take what is formless and void and create a masterpiece.

In Acts 13:2, who birthed the new ministry for Barnabas and Saul?

> **Acts 13:2** And while they were ministering to the Lord and fasting, the Holy Spirit said, "Set apart for Me Barnabas and Saul for the work to which I have called them."

MY ANSWER:

_____

_____

_____

_____

_____

How exciting to see that the Holy Spirit was the one who asked for Saul and Barnabas to be set apart. He is our Commander-in-Chief and He is the one who births new direction for our lives.

Faithful One, does something in your life feel formless and void? What hope do you receive, knowing that the Holy Spirit who lives in you has the role of Creator?

MY ANSWER:

_____

_____

_____

_____

A Friend for the Duration

I remember the first Christmas my father came to visit me in the United States. It seemed like such a long time since the previous summer when my sister and I left him on his own in Hong Kong. I remember walking around with him in New York city. My sister was on one side of him and I was on the other, with our arms in an arm-lock. We paraded through that city like the three musketeers. For that brief week, our burden over the loss of my mother seemed lighter. Somehow, being together made a difference. Together, we could build a new dream for our family.

In John 14:16, what role of the Holy Spirit assures you that you are not alone?

> **John 14:16** "And I will ask the Father, and He will give you another Helper ...

MY ANSWER:

_____

_____

_____

_____

The word for "helper" in the Greek language is "parakletos". It means intercessor or consoler. It has the idea of one coming along side. Notice the word "another" that qualified the noun "helper". This word in the Greek is "allos". It means "another of the same kind". In other words, Jesus is telling us that the Holy Spirit is not someone with different characteristics than Himself. He is "of the same kind".[2] The Holy Spirit in us is like having

Jesus living permanently in us and walking with us on our journey.

In the following verses, listed below, who is the person who shows up consistently?

LIFE STAGES	VERSES
At conception	**Matt 1:18** ...When His mother Mary had been betrothed to Joseph, before they came together she was found to be with child by the Holy Spirit.
At beginning of ministry	**Luke 3:21-23** ... Jesus also was baptized ... and the Holy Spirit descended upon Him in bodily form like a dove ... And when He began His ministry, Jesus Himself was about thirty years
During ministry	**Luke 4:14** And Jesus returned to Galilee in the power of the Spirit...
End of earthly ministry	**Rom 8:11** But if the Spirit of Him who raised Jesus from the dead dwells in you ...

The Apostle Paul tells us in Philippians 1:6, "For I am confident of this very thing, that He who began a good work in you will perfect it ..." In the above verses, we see evidence of this truth. The Holy Spirit is involved in all phases of our lives. He was present when Jesus was conceived. He was present when Jesus was at the beginning of his ministry. He was present during Jesus' ministry. He was present at the end of Jesus' earthly ministry when God destroyed death and raised Jesus from the dead. Whether we are at the beginning or at the end, we can rest assured that God's Holy Spirit will walk with us on our journey.

The End is the Beginning
of Something New

We are children of a Father who had the courage to begin again. Faithful One, where are you in life? Are you at a beginning?

MY ANSWER:

_____

_____

_____

When dreams won't die, search your heart to see if you are obstructing the birth of a new vision. Sometimes, we cling to the past, for fear that burying the dream means burying part of us. The fallacy is to believe that death is the end of all hope. The truth is, we come from a heritage of a Father who has transformed death. Death has no power over us. Ending a dream is not the same as letting a dream die. It simply means that you are allowing God to resurrect your dream in His wonderful, glorious, and spectacular way.

Have the courage to end some things. Some things must end before a new season can begin. I was once in love with a man who could never love me the way I wanted to be loved. Instead of trusting God to lead me into a new future, I continued to hang on, beating my head against the rock to force my dream into a reality. This man was secretly having a number of relationships with women in the different cities that he traveled to. When I discovered his lies, he gave me a song and a dance about how afraid he was of intimacy and that to have a relationship with me, he had to keep these others going at the same time. For a while, I compromised my values, believing in the case he made about his psychological problem. In the end, the relationship fell to pieces and I lost not only the relationship, but part of myself.

Moving Majestically

Sometimes, we hold on to dreams because we are afraid to start all over again. As a result, we prolong our mistakes, trying to make them better, and we blame God when life doesn't turn out the way we want it to. Be honest. What have you been willing to compromise to make your dream a reality?

MY ANSWER:

_____

_____

_____

_____

Remember, God can never work against His own nature. We are the child of the King of Kings. God moves majestically, royally. If we are acting according to our Father's image, we too will move majestically and act royally.

Study Mark 10:17-22 and answer the following questions.

> **Mark 10:17-22** ... "Good teacher," he asked, "what must I do to inherit eternal life?" "Why do you call me good?" Jesus answered. "No one is good– except God alone. You know the commandments: 'Do not murder, do not commit adultery, do not steal, do not give false testimony, do not defraud, honor your father and mother.'" "Teacher," he declared, "all these I have kept since I was a boy." Jesus looked at him and loved him. "One thing you lack," he said. "Go, sell everything you have and give to the poor, and you will have treasure in heaven. Then come, follow me." At this the man's face fell. He went away sad, because he had great wealth.

What did Jesus ask for in His relationships?

MY ANSWER:

_____

_____

_____

What did Jesus do when He didn't get what He asked for?

MY ANSWER:

_____

_____

_____

Identify some key relationships in your life such as a spouse, a best friend, someone who used to be an important part of your life. In your dealings with this person, how have you set the boundaries in the relationship?

MY ANSWER:

_____

_____

_____

_____

First of all, let's look at what eternal life is. This was what the man was asking Jesus, "What must I do to inherit eternal life?" Doesn't "eternal life" lead to living in the presence of God forever? So, in His answer, Jesus is telling the man what it will take for him to have a permanent relationship with God. In other words, Jesus is defining the relationship. Jesus is saying, "This is how I want to be loved." The man walked away. Look at what Jesus did. He stood as a King. He did not grovel, and He did not change the rules.

Dancing into the Future
with a Full Emotional Reservoir

In John 16:28-32, from which relationship did Jesus draw His strength?

> **John 16:28-32** I came from the Father and entered the world; now I am leaving the world and going back to the Father.... a time is coming, and has come, when you will be scattered, each to his own home. You will leave me all alone. Yet I am not alone, for my Father is with me. "I have told you these things, so that in me you may have peace. In this world you will have trouble. But take heart! I have overcome the world."

MY ANSWER:

_____

_____

_____

God is the only one who can fill our emptiness completely. When we look to other people to fill the void in our lives, we will find ourselves possessing them and we grow increasingly jealous when they do not reciprocate our affections. We are like a young child who is holding a tiny bird tightly in her hands. In her fear of losing what she loves, she ends up squeezing the little bird to death. Our ability to let go comes from knowing God holds us in His everlasting arms.

In "Why Is Her Life Better Than Mine?" Judith Couchman said, "... When we're overtly jealous, it may be we're unable to individuate ourselves. That is, we're incapable of accepting our value as a separate individual. Our identity is wrapped up in, and totally dependent on, somebody else ... Ironically, uncontrolled jealousy eventually turns on the beloved. We grow bitter toward the person who doesn't meet our every need, our every expectation for an intimate or exclusive relationship ... We become irritated with our children who would rather play with friends than spend time with us ... As with envy, we lack confidence in who we are, in who God made us to be... If we allow it, we can use jealousy to throw us back to dependence on God. The threat of real or imagined loss can cause us to rediscover Him as our only source of security, as the only One who can't be consumed by our jealous pursuit. Putting God in His rightful place – at the center of our hearts – is the key to conquering jealousy." [3]

Faithful One, who have you been depending on to feed your emotional need? Whose acceptance have you been seeking? Through whom have you been trying to define yourself?

MY ANSWER:

_____

_____

_____

God had to teach me who I was. When I finally began living who I was, I found that the way I related to others changed dramatically. The following was a story I wrote after God transformed my self image:

Trading Places

There he was again. He always appears out of nowhere and when I least expected him. I watched him coming closer and every part of me screamed to run the other way. But I stayed and I felt myself slowly backing up against a wall.

"He's not safe", I told myself, "He will take your deepest secrets and use your weaknesses against you. You will trample on your vulnerabilities and you will never feel safe again." And then I became angry because the honest truth was, "I still wanted him in my life."

By now, he was standing right in front of me with a sheepish grin, as one possessing all the power. He took my hand. I stiffened and said, "Don't do this." "Don't do what?" he asked casually, "I love you". With one smooth sweep, he swung me into his arms. My eyes searched his face. Oh, how I wanted to believe him. And then I was disgusted with myself for needing to believe so badly that someone could love me.

The closer he got, the more I remembered. This was not the first time. I had believed him before and I had been totally deceived. "No!" I screamed and pulled away. Tears began to stream down my face. He was not convinced. With all the strength in me, I said, "I need you to ..." The battle was raging within. "Oh," I cried silently, "I need you to love me and not manipulate me." "You need what?" he said, obviously relishing in the control he had over me emotionally. I took a deep breath and answered, "I need you to go away." I pushed him from me and started to walk the other way. My knees felt weak. My body was trembling. "Oh please don't come after me," I begged quietly, "Please don't come after me or else I might weaken and believe the illusion that you could possibly be kind." Surprisingly, he did-n't say a word and so, I kept walking.

When I got home, I fell on my bed. I missed him already. I wrapped my arms around myself in my loneliness. "Stop it!" I rep-rimanded myself, "Get yourself together!" But all I could do was to weep. I felt that a part of me had died. Would I ever live again? Would I ever dare to dream again?

And then the Lord God said, "Daughter of a King, how have you fallen so low? You have allowed a scoundrel to rob you of your dignity. Look into my face and rediscover who you are. Remember what I breathed into your being the day I made you. You are royalty, from the top of your head to the tip of your toes. Look into my face and remember." And I looked up and there in all His glory was my Father, the King of Kings. He was clothed in light and the angels circled His throne and sang, "Glory! Glory! Glory!" As I drew closer, His light burnt away my rags and then like an X-ray, it began to penetrate into the very core of my being. Inch by inch, His light permeated and burnt till the dark-ness fell off, the bleeding evaporated, the wounds healed over and vanished, and what was missing in my soul was perfectly fused into Him and was completed by Him.

"Daughter of a King," He said, "Rise up and take your appoint-ed place on my earth and in my kingdom. You have traded your soul for a lie but I have bought it back for you. You have settled for a love built on emotion that comes and goes like wheat chaff that scatters in the wind. I created you for more. You are heiress to a love that is built on a decision, my decision to give you all that is mine and to give it with such sincerity that I gave my life to protect what I have bequeathed to you. You have run after a union that is fleeting. You have tried to possess a shadow. But, Daughter of a King, I your Father am not a shadow. I am light and in my light, you will find your union. Look in my face and see.

See me and then you will see yourself."

It was as if a veil had been removed from my eyes. How could I have been so blind? The world was enticing me with a romance that was made up in Hollywood. The world was toying with the deepest cravings in my soul, dangling a carrot in front of me, promising but never able to deliver. As I stared into His glory, I saw my utter stupidity. How could I have imagined that the glory He had given me could ever find its union in the glory of anything other than He Himself? I am the child of God, the daughter of a King. Yesterday was a lie. My Father came for me to destroy the lie. He came for me because I belong to Him and Him alone. "Fool!" I said, "Never again. I will receive what is rightfully mine." I stood up and the shackles fell off. I stood up with all the dignity that belonged to me. I stood up and walked with my Father into the future, as a child of God, chosen and anointed by His hand alone. No longer will I grovel and beg and plead for a crumb. My Father has prepared me a feast. I will walk with my head raised high, with authority, with perfect security, with dignity as one who has found her perfect union only in He who is perfect. I was created in the image of my Father and I will not settle for anyone who will not honor me with the honor my Father intended for me when He first made me.

Trusting God to Work Out
His Dream for us His way ...

God delights in giving us the dreams He planted in our hearts. We confuse ourselves when we equate the "what" of a dream with the "how" of a dream. We can tell God our desires but He wants to write the script.

In 1 Chronicles 28:11-12, who gave David the detail plan for his dream to build the temple?

1 Chr 28:11-12 Then David gave his son Solomon the plans for the portico of the temple, its buildings, its storerooms, its upper parts, its inner rooms and the place of atonement. He gave him the plans of all that the Spirit had put in his mind for the courts of the temple of the LORD and all the surrounding rooms, for the treasuries of the temple of God and for the treasuries for the dedicated things.

MY ANSWER:

God gives us our dreams but He chooses to fulfill our dreams His way. In 1 Chronicles 22:5, what was David's evaluation of the person whom God chose to build the temple in his stead? How did David choose to respond?

1 Chr 22:5 David said, "My son Solomon is young and inexperienced, and the house to be built for the LORD should be of great magnificence and fame and splendor in the sight of all the nations. Therefore I will make preparations for it." So David made extensive preparations before his death.

MY ANSWER:

Notice that David's honest evaluation was that he was a better candidate than Solomon. His son, Solomon was "young and inexperienced". Notice, however, that David did not withdraw in resentment. Instead he accepted God's place for him in history. He was chosen to bring peace to the kingdom and Solomon was the one to build the temple in a time of peace. David's dream was to build the temple for God's glory. Therefore, it didn't matter to him whether he received the credit for the job. Instead of hoarding the glory for himself, David responded to the need and determined to help Solomon as much as he could.

What about you, Faithful One? You can test whether your dream is born from God's heart or from your own by seeing how you respond when you don't get to implement your ideas the way you envisioned. If your dream has the opportunity to be fulfilled by someone else, how would you respond? Would you resent that you personally were not chosen to implement the plan? Would you grieve over not being chosen for the job or would you rejoice that the plan will be implemented?

MY ANSWER:

_____

_____

_____

_____

Study the verses of Acts, listed below, and answer the following questions.

Acts 19:19-21 A number who had practiced sorcery brought their scrolls together and burned them publicly. When they calculated the value of the scrolls, the total came to fifty thousand drachmas. In this way the word of the Lord spread widely and grew in power. After all this had happened, Paul decided to go to Jerusalem, passing through Macedonia and Achaia. "After I have been there," he said, "I must visit Rome also."

Acts 21:30-33 The whole city was aroused, and the people came running from all directions. Seizing Paul, they dragged him from the temple, and immediately the gates were shut. While they were trying to kill him, news reached the commander of the Roman troops that the whole city of Jerusalem was in an uproar. He at once took some officers and soldiers and ran down to the crowd. When the rioters saw the commander and his soldiers, they stopped beating Paul. The commander came up and arrested him and ordered him to be bound with two chains ...

Acts 23:11 The following night the Lord stood near Paul and said, "Take courage! As you have testified about me in Jerusalem, so you must also testify in Rome."

Acts 28:16 When we got to Rome, Paul was allowed to live by himself, with a soldier to guard him.

Do you think Paul's dream to go to Rome was fulfilled his way?
MY ANSWER:

_____

_____

_____

What was Paul's ultimate goal?
MY ANSWER:

_____

_____

_____

Study the verses in Acts 20 and Acts 21, listed below and answer the following questions:

Acts 20:22-24 "And now, compelled by the Spirit, I am going to Jerusalem, not knowing what will happen to me there. I only know that in every city the Holy Spirit warns me that prison and hardships are facing me. However, I consider my life worth nothing to me, if only I may finish the race and complete the task the Lord Jesus has given me– the task of testifying to the gospel of God's grace.

Acts 21:8-15 Leaving the next day, we reached Caesarea ... After we had been there a number of days, a prophet named Agabus came down from Judea. Coming over to us, he took Paul's belt, tied his own hands and feet with it and said, "The Holy Spirit says, 'In this way the Jews of Jerusalem will bind the owner of this belt and will hand him over to the Gentiles.'" When we heard this, we and the people there pleaded with Paul not to go up to Jerusalem. Then Paul answered, "Why are you weeping and breaking my heart? I am ready not only to be bound, but also to die in Jerusalem for the name of the Lord Jesus." When he would not be dissuaded, we gave up and said, "The Lord's will be done." After this, we got ready and went up to Jerusalem.

Why was Paul able to accept God's plan for him? What emotions influenced how he responded to life?

MY ANSWER:

_____

_____

_____

_____

_____

What desire drives your life?

MY ANSWER:

_____

_____

_____

_____

Notice that Paul's priority was in completing the work that God gave him to do. His circumstances were not as important to him as "testifying to the gospel of God's grace". Towards that end, Paul was willing not only to be "bound, but also to die in Jerusalem for the name of the Lord Jesus". It was in Jerusalem that Paul was arrested and sent in chains to Rome.

Notice, too, that in Rome, Paul was under house arrest. The only people he could evangelize were those who visited him in prison. Can you imagine Paul, the go-getter, being forced to sit and wait for the opportunity to evangelize? Definitely, his situation forced him to operate in a way that was inconsistent with his temperament.

When God called me out of corporate America, I had a hard time adjusting to being at home because I was so used to deadlines and deliverables. When I read books on temperaments, I could make a tight case for going to work, telling God that I was the kind of person who needed structure. I also needed to be around people. In spite of my protests, I could never sense God's green light. On hindsight, I realize that it was during my time of isolation that God was preparing me for His ministry. Never in a million years would I have expected to be Founder and President of Inspire Women. Today, God has given me back the structure and the people relations that I longed for, but I have learned that God sometimes works against our temperament when something far more important than our immediate satisfaction is at stake.

Faithful One, will you trust God with your life? Will you allow Him to work out your dream His way? In one or two sentences, write out your dream.

MY ANSWER:

_____

_____

_____

_____

Now, evaluate what you have written. Are you telling God the "what" of your dream or are you specifying the "how"? How would you restate your dream in terms that allows God the freedom to determine how your dream will be fulfilled? (For example, if you have a strong nurturing instinct, you might have said, "I wish to be married and have six kids". To restate your dream in a way that gives God the freedom to determine the "how" might be, "I wish to glorify God in a way that uses my desire to nurture others. Having family is one possibility but I am not going to limit God by my preconceptions on how things must work out.")

MY ANSWER:

_____

_____

Living on God's Eternal Timeline ...

God delights in fulfilling the dreams He planted in our hearts, but He wants to fulfill the dream His way. God also wants to fulfill the dream in His time. Remember, God doesn't function on the same time line that we do. God has an eternal time line.

In Philippians 1:6, Paul said, "being confident of this, that he who began a good work in you will carry it on to completion until the day of Christ Jesus." Don't limit God by the temporary breath of life that you have on this earth. His dream will be fulfilled in you. He who began a good work in you will complete it, but He will carry it on to completion until the day of Christ Jesus. For many of us, our biggest dream may be fulfilled when Jesus comes back to earth and carries us to the other side of eternity.

When you trusted in the name of Jesus, God grafted you into an eternal time line. God has a dream for your life. Your challenge and mine is to believe in our Father's character and to know that we will be operating at our potential, some time in our eternal life span. To force God to give us results on this side of eternity is to put a human-made artificial timeframe on a God who has an eternal timeline.

When God's Dream for us Becomes Bigger than Ourselves

In the class I taught to help women reach their potential, God taught me so much through the lives of these gifted women. One of the women in the class, Sharon Radionoff, has a P.H.D. in music and is one of eight people in this nation who is specifically trained to care for professional and injured voices. As a singing voice specialist, she uses her knowledge of human anatomy and physiology to produce the best sound in a way that protects the health of the client's vocal chords. When Sharon first came to the class, we spent hours talking about her vision. She was so sure that God meant for her to be affiliated with a

University or with an Ear, Nose, and Throat Doctor who specializes in care of the voice. Instead, God opened the way for her to start her own company.

As we talked about how her vision developed into the "Sound Singing Institute", I said to her, "What kept you from going out on your own?" She said, "I have always heard that starting a business is a risky business and I was afraid that I would not be able to pay my bills." As she and I talked, we realized that a vision becomes a reality when the vision grows to become bigger than ourselves. At some point, we stop worrying about our personal needs and the risks our vision will cost us. Instead, the dream drives and consumes us and we finally realize that we have been given a part in something bigger than ourselves. You see, the dream belongs to God and was born in His heart and is part of an eternal agenda.

As the breath of heaven breathes through our body, we become sure that when we pursue what is bigger than ourselves, the mundane details of our personal needs will take care of themselves. We begin to see the miracle that happens when we put God's dream first. In Matthew 6:31-33, Jesus said, "So do not worry, saying, 'What shall we eat?' or 'What shall we drink?' or 'What shall we wear?' For the pagans run after all these things, and your heavenly Father knows that you need them. But seek first his kingdom and his righteousness, and all these things will be given to you as well." – We see that when we pursue the dream God has put in our hearts over and above our concern with how the dream will benefit us personally, we are free from the chains that bind us; and for the first time in our lives, we are free to fly as high as the wind of God's Spirit takes us.

A Dot is Just a Dot Until ...

In Genesis 1:1, God's Word to us begins with this message, " In the beginning God created the heavens and the earth." Have you ever asked yourself, "In the beginning of what?" Whose beginning are we talking about?

MY ANSWER:

_____

_____

_____

We know we're not talking about the beginning of God because God has no beginning. In the space below, take a moment to study God's timeline. Observe a horizontal line that represents a timeline. On the left end of the line is an arrow facing left, to represent eternity past. At the right end of the line is an arrow facing right, to represent eternity future. Now think about the span of your life and plot your life on God's timeline. What does your life look like?

GOD'S TIMELINE

← _____ →

ETERNITY PAST   ETERNITY FUTURE

If you plotted your life like I did, you would have a microscopic dot on God's eternal timeline. So, let me ask you this question, "How significant is one life in the scheme of things?" Yet, is there any doubt that God sees us as significant. How do we get our significance?

MY ANSWER:

_____

_____

_____

Oh Faithful One, don't you see? The only time our lives become significant is when we align ourselves with where God is going. We are just a dot. God is the one with an eternal timeline. When we align ourselves with where God is going, that is the moment when the dot of our lives become transformed into a life with eternal significance.

Faithful One, God has a dream for your life. When you take your eyes off yourself, you will see that though you have been appointed to be God's dream bearer, the dream is much bigger than you. When you see no hope for a dream to be fulfilled, then raise your vision higher. Will you have the courage to lay your temporal dream on the altar and trust God to resurrect it with the breath of eternity? God wants your dream transformed by Him. God wants His hope in place of your disappointment. God desires to give you a dream empowered by His Spirit, shaped by His image, pulsating with His life, guaranteed by His character to give you more than you could ask or imagine for yourself. Will you exchange your story for God's greater story which He wants to tell through your life?

Jesus said, in John 15:16, "You did not choose me, but I chose you and appointed you to go and bear fruit– fruit that will last ...". In Jeremiah 17:7-10, God says, "... blessed is the man who trusts in the LORD, whose confidence is in him. He will be like a tree planted by the water that sends out its roots by the stream. It does not fear when heat comes; its leaves are always green. It has no worries in a year of drought and never fails to bear fruit." Notice that when we trust our lives in God's hands, He assures us that even when our circumstances put us in a year of drought, we will still flourish and bear fruit. Do you believe God's Word? Then receive it and celebrate with God into your future.

May you plant your life on a great heritage and soar higher than an eagle. May you receive the full power of His anointing, burn with His inextinguishable flame, live expectantly in life's waiting places, trust in His character, accept His choices and celebrate the perfect satisfaction of a dream, resurrected with the breath of heaven. Oh may you exchange the stirring and groaning in your heart for an eternal flame that will overcome the darkness with His magnificent splendor and glory!

PART IV

Inspire Women Staff Who Persevered In Their Calling

God established Inspire Women to help women to connect their lives with His purpose and to fund their training for ministry. Our marching orders required a staff that was willing to lay down their personal dreams in order to invest in the potential of others to change the world with the power of God's Word.

I would like to share with you some of the testimonies of the women on staff at Inspire Women. These testimonies were selected because I have observed these women over a long term period and have witnessed their faithfulness to work tirelessly beside me during our hardest challenges. These women have worked hours into the night without any complaint. They have embraced their calling as a privilege and blessing. They have met deadlines and finished the task while trusting God to provide the resources. They selflessly give to others while trying to cover their own support. When given the opportunity to leave for easier conditions, they chose to remain by my side to finish the work God entrusted to us. In this chapter, I pray you will be encouraged by the testimonies of Mia Kang, Joan Turley, and Barbara Govan.

Mia Kang's Testimony

Mia came to Inspire Women and served under our Sold-Out Singles Program. The Sold-Out Singles program was a program where we selected women from a national search, who demonstrated evidence of success in corporate America and were willing to walk away from their careers to use their skills to build an eternal kingdom. After seven months with Inspire Women, Mia was promoted to Chief Operating Officer and Development Executive. Whatever dream God entrusts to Inspire Women, Mia is the logistics person who makes sure we're on track and make our deadlines. Mia gave the following testimony at the end of a series I was teaching around the city titled, "Living in the Miraculous". I pray her testimony will bless you in a special way.

In January of 2004, I (Mia Kang) was listening to Anita Carman teach the word of God, and I remember feeling like I was at a point in my life, where I would do anything for God.

And then, I got a phone call at work, it was Anita, and she wanted to know what I thought about this idea she had, called the Sold-Out Singles Program. She wanted to know if I thought it would be exciting to live in an apartment with a bunch of sold out single women for God, serving the community. I was speechless. For one I had never spoken to Anita before, and I was in shock that she had called me. Secondly, I didn't think her idea sounded very appealing, and I didn't know how to tell her that. I just said God had not put that kind of vision in my heart, and hung up the phone as quickly as I could. You see, I had just come to the point with God where I realized that I needed to be praying about marriage; my whole church and family had come to this point long before me, and always prays for my future husband. So, I thought this could not be from God. But shortly after we hung up, I started feeling like I may have discouraged Anita;

She seemed so excited on the phone. So, I sent her an email, explaining to her why God had not put that vision in my heart. Well she calls me back, laughing, and assures me that she was not trying to turn me into a nun, and wanted to know if I could come and talk to her that night.

HINDRANCE 1 – LOGIC

So there I was sitting in her office, listening to her tell me about the vision of Inspire and the Sold-Out Singles Program, and it was everything I was passionate about. I was already doing similar things on a smaller scale, and I felt like God was preparing me for something like this IN THE FUTURE, but I couldn't believe that God would call me out right now, I wasn't ready. I tried to tell Anita and God that due to my circumstances, it would not be logical for me to do this right now.

It isn't logical to quit a good paying job, to raise my own financial support, which would be 4 times less than my current salary! It isn't logical to make less, when I'm trying to pay off my school loan, it would take way too long to pay off. And it isn't logical right now, because I don't know if my father is a believer, and he already thinks I'm a Jesus freak. This would take him over the edge, and possibly turn him off from God even more.

Seeing my parents living for the Lord is my heart's desire, and it is also very important to me to be able to financially bless them, especially now that they are getting older. In the Asian culture children are expected to take care of their parents, and being that I am the only one with a college degree, and knowing all the sacrifices they made for me to have higher education and a good paying job, they were hoping and I was hoping I would be able to bless them in their old age. It was really hard for me to trust God with taking care of my parents spiritually and physically.

What I hadn't realized, while I was sitting in Anita's class, feeling like I could do anything for God, was that I felt like I could do anything so long as it was humanly possible. And this condition is fine, when "I" do something for God, but when GOD does something through me, it's not going to be humanly possible, it is miraculous.

HINDRANCE 2 – THE COST

My second issue was the cost. I enjoyed being "blessed to be a blessing". And it was easy for me to give, because I had a lot, but the real test comes when I don't have much. This offer to come to Inspire was God's way of asking me to give at my own expense, and the cost wasn't just monetary, but it was also laying down my dreams and my desires. And selfishly, I felt like I had already laid down enough. And then I realized that this wasn't just about Inspire, I felt the real question God was asking me was, "Would I still follow Him if it cost me everything? Not mostly everything, not more than so and so, but everything?"

I struggled for weeks about this, I couldn't eat or sleep. I remember crying on the phone with Anita still trying to convince her, I was not the person for this position. I remember telling her, I don't feel sold out to Christ, because I am struggling with this decision. And she encouraged me by reminding me, struggling doesn't determine whether or not you are sold out, it's how you choose in the struggle. So one night, I did what every good Christian is not supposed to do, I opened my bible and looked to the very first verse that caught my attention for guidance, and here's what it said:

Mark 10:29 "I tell you the truth, Jesus replied, "No one who has left home or brothers or sisters or mother or father or children or fields for me and the Gospel will fail to receive a hundred times as much in this present age (......and with them, persecutions) and in the age to come, eternal life."

Whatever we do for God will be given back to us a hundred times in this present age and in the age to come, here I am holding onto crumbs when God has greater things for me. I was letting Satan go to work on me. I was so focused on me and what I thought I was losing, that I lost sight of who God is. He is way more generous and gracious and loving to me than I could ever be to Him or anyone else. In that moment I told God that I would do His will no matter what. I called Anita the next day, and accepted the offer. I didn't know how I was going to pay for my school loan, what would happen with my relationship with my parents, I didn't have all the answers, I just had God's peace.

THE MIRACLES – THE MONEY

The day I said yes to the offer, God provided for one of the biggest things holding me back from taking this position, my school loan. A friend I hadn't spoken to in a long time called me, and I had the chance to share with him about Inspire and my decision to leave the corporate world. The next day he emailed me and said he felt led to pay my monthly school loan payments for the next 7 months, without even knowing my payment amount or me asking him to do this. He shared with me in his email that he had just started trying to spend time with God again, and in His quiet time he felt God wanted him to do this.

God also gave me the support of my church. I received great encouragement from my pastor and his wife. They allowed me to go before the congregation and ask for financial support from the body of Christ, and the congregation gave me exactly the amount I needed.

Then there was my company, I asked them for an extended leave of absence. Technically I should have been terminated after 3 months, but they allowed me to stay on leave of absence for my 7 month commitment with Inspire, and I was able to keep all my benefits. I told them there was a huge possibility I would not return, and they knew I was leaving to serve God, and they still gave me their blessing. They also paid me out for all my vacation time, which was a huge answer to prayer, because before I could go before my church and ask them for their financial support, I had to show my own personal sacrifice by giving 20% of my total support from my own pocket, which I didn't have. The vacation check I received from my company was a little over 20% of my total support. God also gave me the courage to ask the chairman of my company to buy a table at our fundraiser Luncheon; and he did.

MY PARENTS

Then the last obstacle was my parents, they thought I had gone insane, and would not bless my decision to do this, and their blessing was very important to me. We finally came to a compromise. They agreed to bless my decision if I agreed to go back to the corporate world after my 7 month commitment at Inspire was over, to think about things for a year. If after a year, I still felt called to full time ministry, they would bless my decision. This was a huge step for them, and I thought this was a miracle too, so I agreed.

Well, when my 7 month commitment was coming to an end, Anita asked me if I would stay on longer. This time the decision making process was very different. I had finally come to a point, where I trusted God with my dreams and my provisions, because I had experienced the miraculous, and I survived.

But there was one problem with me staying at Inspire, that Anita and I both knew, the promise to my parents that I would go back to the corporate world to "think" about things more clearly. She and I both agreed that in order for me to stay, my parents would have to release me from my promise. Things weren't looking good. The day I went to talk to my Dad, he went irate before I could even finish telling him my story. He even started throwing things, so I took that as my cue to leave, and I told Anita the next day, that it didn't look like my parents would be changing their mind. Yet, for some reason I felt like God was about to do a miracle, everything looked bleak, but there was this burning in my heart from God, that said, "Don't you recognize me? Do you see that I am in this?" I went back 2 days later to talk to my parents again and when I walked into the house, I felt like I had entered the twilight zone. My parents reacted completely differently. For the first time in my entire life my mother suggested they should let me do what I want to do, and my Dad agreed. These two rarely agree on anything, and here they were blessing something they were so adamantly against.

I called Anita and told her I would commit to Inspire for as long as God wanted me there. Soon after a donor stepped in and underwrote the Inspire organization. We would no longer have to raise our own support, and we could focus our energy on teaching and ministering to the women and raising an endowment to ensure the funds would always be there to inspire and to train women for ministry.

God gives us back a hundred times in this age and the age to come. I know there are more trials and tribulations to come, and I need to let go of a lot more than I even realize, but I am striving to say, "I consider everything a loss compared to the surpassing greatness of knowing Christ Jesus my Lord, for whose sake I have lost all things. I consider them rubbish, that I may gain Christ, Phil 3:8."

Joan Turley's Testimony

Joan Turley began at Inspire Women as Anita Carman's personal assistant. She served faithfully and was there for Anita not only as an assistant but as a friend. Over time, Anita observed that Joan has an exceptional gift in relating to women and in helping them to believe in what God can do through them. She also has a creative side that is perfectly suited to creating special events. So, Anita moved Joan into the position of Director of Community Relations and Special Projects.

I (Joan Turley) love stories. When I am entranced in a really good story the world around me fades away and I am transported to another time and place where I live vicariously through the story of the hero. In story, I am knighted as a warrior princess, I conquer villains and vanquish every foe and tragedy finds meaning in my destiny. The power of story has filled my days as far back as I can remember. Therefore, is it any wonder that God has used HIS–story to help me find significance in the heartbreak of life?

This is my story…well, its part of my story, for He has not yet finished writing the script of my life, but I pray that it will bless you and help you to more fully trust the One who authors your life as you journey toward our Father's home.

I have been asked to share with you how I came to be a part of the Inspire Women team. In trying to recall all the many steps that led me to Inspire Women I found myself sitting quietly before the Lord and asking Him, "Lord, how do I explain this journey that you have called me to?" To that question He simply replied, "Whitewater Rafting", and then He reminded me of an incredible teaching moment I had on a white water adventure.

Seventeen years ago, I vacationed on the American River. During the early morning hours, before my family awakened, I'd make my way outdoors to enjoy the beauty of the river, nestled in those California Mountains. Even now, when I am very still, if I close my eyes and remember those days, I can hear the roar of that river and I can see the sunlight as it dances on the water.

I vividly remember my first morning on the river. I was sitting quietly, listening to the roar of the river and just breathing in the beauty around me, when the solitude of the morning was broken by a steady stream of river riders. One by one, they came ... kayakers, canoers and rafters all swiftly paddling by. The thrill of adventure was written on their faces, they were caught up in the moment, they were focused, they were passionate, they were intense, they were involved, body, mind and soul. This was the adventure of a lifetime and they were completely immersed in the moment.

For days I watched those river riders navigate the rapids and soon a group of us began to talk about riding the river too. I began to imagine what it would be like to ride that river wild. Listening to the locals, I heard the stories of those who lost their lives for the thrill of the ride, yet still the river began to call and I found myself no longer content to just wade on the river banks, all I could think of was "Could I ride this river...Could I really do it....Did I have it in me to ride the white water?" My emotions were crazy...I teetered between absolute fear and extreme courage. There was a tug of war going on inside my heart and head. But finally, I decided I would ride that river and there would be no turning back.

When the big day came, I kissed my children good-bye and donned my river-gear. I got in the boat and trusted my life to the river guide. Well sort of. I was too scared to take a side rowing position, so I sat in the middle of the raft and held on for dear life. As the river guide called out the commands, "Everyone lean to the right or everyone lean to the left or paddle, paddle, paddle, hard left, hard right," I would scream out his commands over and over again, as if no one else was paying attention.

As we hit the first white water my adrenaline was pumping and I was screaming the guide's commands to everyone in the boat. The ride through our first rapid was fast and hard, but before I knew it we were safely through. I looked back over my shoulder and breathed a deep sigh of relief, and then I took another deep breath and started screaming the guide's commands all over again. This went on for hours, (I don't know how the rest of the people in the boat put up with me) till at last the "troublemaker", a class four white water rapid was in our line of vision.

Everything else up to this point had been child's play. This was it, this was the big test, and this was what we had been preparing for all day. This was the spot on the river where people lose their lives every year. And now here I was sitting in this raft, and all I could think of was, "What in the world have I done? Oh Lord Jesus, help me to be strong." At this point, there was nothing for me to do but hang on and scream the river guide's commands as loud as I possibly could. And that's exactly what I did. And then wow...what a ride it was...it was the scariest thing I had ever done and yet it was the most amazing adventure I had ever been a part of. I loved it so much I did it again the very next day...the river had called my name and I was hooked....I had to follow.

You see, you don't really appreciate the thrill of the ride, till you look back and see what you've come safely through. When I looked back, all I could see was white water; when I looked ahead all I could see were the sidelines of the riverbank filled with spectators – clapping and cheering us onward. We had overcome and the river guide had led us safely through.

Through the white water experience, God taught me that in order to navigate safely through the rapids of life, everything hinges on obeying the commands of the One who guides us through the waters of life. That was a really important lesson for me to learn and that experience became the spring board for future obedience.

Almost six years ago I found myself on another river. But this was a different kind of river; this was a concrete river called the Katy Freeway in Houston, Texas. And this time I wasn't in a boat; I was in car traveling 70 mph racing to church. On the way, I popped in a cassette tape on the subject of prayer, thinking this would be great thing for my teenage kids to hear. However, from the moment that tape began to play, it was as if everything around me faded and it was just me and God and there on that concrete river I began to hear THE RIVER GUIDE calling out His commands to me, "Joan, it's time for you to leave the banks of the river, it's time for you to come out into the deep. It's time for you to stop wading in the shallow waters of little time spent with me. Come out to the deep where the River will carry you."

I remember telling Him, "But God, I don't know how to do this. He said, "Child, you've been on the banks long enough, I've seen your desire to go deeper with me and this is your moment. Will you follow where I am leading?" I said, "Yes, Lord, I will follow where you lead." He said "Child, meet me in the morning and I'll teach you all you need to know." And so began the ride of my life...of following hard the River Guide.

In 2003, about four years into the spiritual discipline of seeking God, I was working for a company that paid well and provided regular raises and bonuses when I sensed God calling me to walk away from my job. There was a sense of urgency about this calling; I felt compelled that I was to step out into an unknown future, much like Abraham. God was asking me to walk away and trust Him completely.

Looking back now, I can see that God used those early days of discipline to prepare me for my walk with Inspire Women.

Those were custom designed training days and He wanted to know that I would be diligent to obey His call in the smallest of details. He used those days of prayer to reconnect me to a passion that had once filled my days.

For you see, at the age of 18, I had surrendered my life to ministry and I spent the first 12 years of my adult life serving on staff with a ministry. But things did not work out the way I had expected and my husband and I found ourselves, wounded, broken and very much floundering, just trying to make sense of it all. We really didn't know what we were to do with our lives; eventually we both found jobs in the secular market. But, I could not escape the sense of God's calling upon my life. I did not realize that when God began to call me to those mornings of prayer, he was reconditioning me, much like an athlete who comes out of retirement to compete again. What a joy it was to realize that after raising two children, God was directing me back into full-time ministry.

Though I was thrilled that God was leading me out of the secular job market and back into some type of full-time ministry, I was also scared to death. I didn't know how we would make ends meet. When I shared with my husband that I sensed God was asking me to walk away from my job and that He had whispered to my soul...He would provide, my husband blessed the calling and in essence said, "Joan, if this is what God is telling you to do, be obedient...God will provide." So, in June of 2003 I resigned from my job and stepped out into the unknown.

I must confess, in those first few weeks of leaving my job, there were moments that I thought maybe I had missed His leading. I remember waking up in the middle of the night, fearful and afraid. My biggest fear was that if I had missed His leading and had made a mistake that I would harm my children's ability to trust in God's leading for their life. I did not want to create a circumstance that would ever hinder their ability to trust the One who calls our name. Though I was unsure of my steps in the beginning, His Spirit led me onward.

Upon leaving my job, God placed one open door before me and so that was the door I walked through. That door was Inspire Women. So, in obedience to His leading I began to volunteer. I had really never done the "volunteer" thing; that was new territory for me. I remember confiding in God and only one other person – my spiritual mom, "If God wants me to come on board with Inspire Women, then this is what I pray, I pray that God will let Anita know that I am to be on staff and she will be the one to extend the invitation for me to become a part of Inspire Women." Well, two months into volunteering, Anita Carman asked me to join her staff and then I knew that God was confirming to me that this was the place He wanted me to plant my feet. It's now been almost two years and I have absolutely loved serving with this ministry and I am ever humbled that God has chosen me to be a part of this team.

Though I am on staff and loving every minute of it, trials still come my way and struggles still remain. God will never allow me to become so comfortable that I no longer need to seek His face. He has the most amazing ways of allowing circumstances to keep drawing me back to Him. For example, as Inspire was closing out the year 2004, Anita felt led of the Lord to have each member of her staff, seek God's direction as to whether or not God would have us continue on the Inspire team. She only wanted a team that was committed and sold out to the mission. I was faced with a decision and I needed to know if God wanted me to stay. And so, I began to struggle to find His heart in the matter.

I spent three weeks agonizing over this decision. Everyday I would ask Him, "Lord, what do you want me to do? Do I stay or do I go? I need an answer and Lord I really want it NOW." It was a difficult struggle. But one morning I awoke to hear His voice whispering in my ear. It was crystal clear, it was as if God was sitting next to me, asking me, "Joan, have I opened another door for you?" and I said "No". He said, "Then, stay the course. I want you to stay the course". And instantly the struggle ended and a peace filled my heart. I had heard from God. I had my marching orders and everything was now in order or so I thought. I boldly announced to Anita, I had my answer; I was staying the course and she would count me in.

I thought everything was going to be smooth sailing. Then, one week later, my former employer called me out of the blue and said, "Joan I need you to come back and work with me." She was forming a new company and wanted me to part of it. I had learned so many good things from my former employer and much of what I contribute to Inspire is because of all that I learned from her. This new development completely rocked my boat! Here I was being presented with another open door, and this open door offered the financial blessings my family greatly needed. Oh my, what was I supposed to do now and the struggle began all over. I had to make another decision. However, praise God, it did not take me long to recognize that this decision could not be based on money, it must be based on His marching orders and the last thing He said to me was, "Stay the course." I called my former boss and told her I needed to follow God's marching orders.

I have learned that when you say "Yes" to God, there will be a test soon afterwards, and most likely the grass will look greener on the other side. God is looking for those who will lay down their dreams to pick up His dreams. Through the story of Inspire Women you have read how God has provided in marvelous and miraculous ways but experiencing the miraculous will require a cost. I pray that my story – our stories have given you the courage to step out in obedience no matter what the cost. May you be blessed in following Him and may your story be a light to those who sit in darkness.

Barbara Govan's Testimony

Barbara Govan serves as Director of Scholarships at Inspire Women. Through her efforts, Inspire Women developed processes to give each scholarship applicant the best opportunity to communicate their ministry interests and potential to a selection panel. Her processes provide an efficient way to evaluate the many applicants that come to Inspire Women while at the same time keeping the personal touch in working with each applicant.

> **Hebrews 11:6 reads**, "And without faith it is impossible to please God, because anyone who comes to him must believe that he exists and that he rewards those who earnestly seek him."

As a child and a young adult, I (Barbara Govan) was timid and shy. I was afraid of everything. I was easily discouraged by the negative comments or actions of others. I would often retreat into myself if my requests were denied. But I found comfort in my home and my family, and I insulated myself from the world through my mother, father and sister. My mother was very outgoing and never met a stranger. My sister had loads of friends, and was a tremendous talker. My father didn't talk much, but he was adventurous. And then there was me. I sheltered myself from the world in order to protect myself from hurt or pain. But God had a different plan for my life, and he introduced it in a whirlwind.

In October 1967 I received a phone call from my college roommate's mother that foretold of events that would change my life and heart forever. The phone rang, and she asked me why I was still there. Now I am in a dorm room in Colorado, and have no plans for returning to Houston until Christmas break. So I'm wondering what is she talking about?

She quickly gets off of the phone and tells me to call home. I call my house, but no one answers. I call my sister, who is now married, and no one answers at her house. I call her in-laws and her mother-in-law answers, and just keeps repeating the phrase, "Lord have mercy, oh you poor thing." Then she tells me to call my sister at my great aunt's house. I finally get through to my sister who tells me that, "Mother and father have been shot." She does not give me any details, and I am too shocked to ask any questions. I immediately begin to pack. Before I can get everything in my luggage, there is a knock on my dorm room. The resident advisor had been contacted by my family, and a student with a car was already prepared to take me immediately to the airport in Denver, which is about an hour's drive. Everybody knows what has happened but me.

On the ride to the airport and on the airplane, I pray that my parents will be all right. These are the two longest rides of my life. I was hoping, "This is just some horrible accident, and that my little sheltered world will go back to being the way it was— safe." When I arrived in Houston, I learned that my father had committed suicide, and in the process he and my mother struggled over the gun, and she was killed as well. All the pain that I had spent years avoiding was now upon me. It's an avalanche! I'm devastated! I can't do anything!

But God is love and goodness and mercy. And through this tragedy He transformed my mind. Just like Job and Joseph, He used my brokenness to train me in the way that He would have me to go. Through this tragedy He helped me to overcome fear, and He gave me a testimony. He let me see first hand who He is, and how He works. And that to me is the miracle; that God came close to me, so that I could know Him – His love for me and His faithfulness.

That was over 35 years ago and the lessons I learned then are still true today. In January of 2004, I found myself with another tough decision. Should I keep working or should I retire? Not working had never crossed my mind, but God dropped the idea in my spirit, and I retired in 2004 after working for the same company for 30 years.

I didn't know it at the time, but God was leading me on another faith walk. I left the security of my salary, co-workers, and the comfort of "familiar work" to step into the unknown.

I'm learning to live off less money and enjoy it. And I'm learning that God is not finished with me yet.

In February 2004, I came to Inspire Women. Anita Carman put me to work immediately, and in an area in which I had no previous experience. I'm learning how a non-profit works. Ministry is not easy. In fact it's harder because you have fewer resources and you attempt deadlines that seem totally unreachable according to your human logic. For example, as Anita is working with the donors, she may need some information on the scholarship applicants that normally takes a week. But Anita will need it the next day. So I am learning how to turn my entire world around to fit into what will serve God's kingdom and timetable. Anita will also trust me with a lot. For instance, she'll say, "Come up with the process to evaluate all the scholarship applicants." I find myself working challenges I have never dealt with before. In dealing with many of our applicants, I had to learn to see life from their perspective. One of the first applications I read, I was ready to throw out the application because it was sloppily done. Anita challenged me to call the applicant. When I did, I found out that some people have a passion for ministry but don't know how to fill out a form. So, part of the scholarship procedure includes my helping each candidate present themselves in the best light to the selection committee. I am learning that God continues to stretch me to have mercy and to respond with His heart.

He is doing a new thing in me because I am asking for His guidance and direction. I am giving up me and taking on the responsibilities that He wants me to have. And the reward is joy in my heart. I urge and encourage you to step out, step out into the deep waters with Jesus. It sounds scary, but it's not! All you need is faith the size of a mustard seed.

And He will teach you like He is doing with me that:

1) God will sometimes allow thorns in our sides to teach us how to grow and to live in spite of them. God did not cause my parents to be killed. My father acted on his own free will and in his wrong choice, it hurt my mother as well as the rest of my family. God is in the deliverance business, and in His mercy, He comes into our lives to heal the pain our wrong choices have caused. He walked beside me day and night until I was able to trust Him with all my heart and lean not unto my own understanding. He moved me from head knowledge to heart knowledge. Sometimes He allows our desperation so we will seek Him with all of our heart.

2) Nothing is more important than spending time in God's Word. I came to a more accurate understanding of God and His work. I learned firsthand that He is THE way, THE truth, and THE light. He is sovereign. When I understood that God is sovereign, I was able to let go of fear of rejection, shame that my father had committed suicide, and doubt that I could go on as an orphan. God became larger than my fears. I could not see HIM or accept His power before because I was too caught up in the world – my family, myself. God became a living being that I could talk to and receive answers from. He gave my heart ease. God is sovereign, and I must place no other God before Him. And when He reveals His will, I must be obedient.

3) I must make a conscious decision to trust God and to act on His Word no matter the circumstances – pain, shame.

Job 13:15 Though he slay me, yet will I hope in him; I will surely [a] defend my ways to his face.

Isaiah 54:17 No weapon forged against you will prevail, and you will refute every tongue that accuses you. This is the heritage of the servants of the LORD, and this is their vindication from me," declares the LORD.

Psalm 23:4 Even though I walk through the valley of the shadow of death, I will fear no evil, for you are with me; your rod and your staff, they comfort me.

4) Stand on His Word and see His miracle-working power first hand. God is a rewarder of those who diligently seek Him. And if thou canst believe, all things are possible to him who believeth. The semester that my parents died, I made all A's in school. I never had to wonder about my tuition. I could look people in the eye, and not feel ashamed that my father had committed suicide and killed my mother. He stilled my heart and gave me peace in the middle of my storm. God freed my mind from being bitter or paralyzed by my losses. Instead, I could share my testimony of how good God is. God provided for all of my needs according to His riches in Christ Jesus. He brought me from sadness to JOY, and He'll do the same for you. Just trust Him!

In retirement, God has provided for all of my needs, and I have not been anxious, but have found peace and joy in being on the battlefield and claiming my blessings.

Endnotes

PART 1

1. **PAGE 197** – DISAPPOINTMENT WITH GOD, Philip Yancey, page 57. Copyright © 1988-1994. Zondervan Publishing House, Grand Rapids, Michigan.

2. **Page 198-199** – WHEN GOD DOESN'T MAKE SENSE, Dr. James Dobson, page 13. Copyright © 1993. Tyndale House Publishers, Inc. Used by permission. All rights reserved.

PART 3

1. **Page 223** – Taken from: THEOLOGICAL WORDBOOK OF THE OLD TESTAMENT, by R. Laird Harris, Gleason L. Archer, Jr., and Bruce K. Waltke, pages 505, 430. Copyright © 1980, Moody Bible Institute of Chicago. Moody Press. Used by permission.

2. **Page 224** – WORD STUDIES OF THE HOLY SPIRIT, E. W. Bullinger, page 61. Published by Kregel Publications, Grand Rapids, Michigan, 1979.

3. **Page 229** – WHY IS HER LIFE BETTER THAN MINE?, Judith Couchman, (Colorado Springs, Colorado: Navpress Books & Bible Studies, 1991), pages 27-28.